STUDIES IN HISTORY, ECONOMICS, AND PUBLIC LAW

EDITED BY THE FACULTY OF POLITICAL SCIENCE
OF COLUMBIA UNIVERSITY

Number 280

FOOD COSTS AND CITY CONSUMERS

Significant Factors in Metropolitan Distribution of Perishables

FOOD COSTS AND CITY CONSUMERS

Significant Factors in Metropolitan Distribution of Perishables

BY

CHARLES ENOS ARTMAN, Ph.D.

Formerly Research Agent in Marketing
U. S. Department of Agriculture

NEW YORK
COLUMBIA UNIVERSITY PRESS
1926

Copyright, 1926
by
CHARLES ENOS ARTMAN

PRINTED IN THE UNITED STATES OF AMERICA

PREFACE

Economical distribution of the food supply is a subject of vital concern alike to consumers dwelling in great population centers, and to the body of producers throughout the nation. The Joint Commission of Agricultural Inquiry reported in 1921 its conviction that distribution is one of the most important economic problems before the American people, and that only through its solution can adequate adjustments be made among agriculture, industry, transportation, labor, finance and commerce. The machinery of distribution requires adjustment in order that the outlay of the final consumer may be related more closely to what the producer receives for his products. The wide gap between producers' receipts and consumers' outlays results in large measure from intermediate handling costs arising after goods arrive in the city wholesale markets. Yet comparatively little detailed or systematic study has been given to these factors of city distribution.

In the present work detailed consideration is given to some factors in the expense of distribution under conditions typical of the New York metropolitan area. Fresh fruits and vegetables are particularly appropriate for this study because of the prominent place which they generally hold in family expenditures, because the problem of distribution is intensified by their perishable nature, and because efficient methods of handling such goods are more essential than with less perishable commodities.

This study was undertaken early in 1923 under the joint auspices of the United States Bureau of Agricultural Economics and the Port of New York Authority, as one of a series of inquiries into terminal handling costs. The work of collecting and analyzing the data was undertaken and executed by the author under the general supervision of Walter P. Hedden, of the joint research staff of the two agencies. The statistical tabulations were made by the machine tabulating section of the Bureau of Agricultural Economics in Washington. The illustrations are reproduced from United States Department of Agriculture Bulletin 1411, through the courtesy of Mr. J. Clyde Marquis, Director of Economic Information.

For valuable assistance in the large amount of careful statistical analysis involved in this work, special acknowledgment is given to H. D. Comer, former Research Agent in Marketing and now with the Bureau of Business Research of Ohio State University.

For aid in obtaining the information here presented, acknowledgment is due to numerous persons and agencies in the metropolitan area. Proprietors of individual retail stores, officials of chain-store systems, and dealers in the wholesale and jobbing markets of New York, Brooklyn and Newark gave invaluable assistance by supplying regular price quotations and market information for an extended period. Particular credit is given to the public-spirited women who submitted regular reports of prices in their neighborhood stores from week to week. The following civic and educational agencies gave active assistance in enlisting reporters for this work: Women's City Club of New York, New York League of Women Voters, Teachers College of Columbia University, Henry Street Settlement, Pratt Institute of Brooklyn, Civitas Club of Brooklyn, Brooklyn Society of Ethical Culture, Contemporary Club of Newark, Women's Club of Elizabeth, Housewives' Economic League of Passaic.

The author acknowledges his indebtedness also to Professor E. R. A. Seligman, Wesley C. Mitchell, Paul H. Nystrom, O. S. Morgan, and Frederick C. Mills, of Columbia University, each of whom examined the manuscript and contributed constructive suggestions.

While this work is restricted to a few specific factors of metropolitan distribution, it shows quite positively the influence of consumers' buying habits on distribution expenses. This demonstration is significant not alone in the marketing of perishable foodstuffs, but in the distribution of all commodities that are sold in variable small-quantity units.

CHARLES E. ARTMAN.

COLUMBIA UNIVERSITY, MAY 21, 1926.

CONTENTS

CHAPTER I

Importance of Metropolitan System of Food Distribution

Nearly one-twelfth of the total population of the United States lives and works in the New York metropolitan area, in the territory included roughly within a radius of thirty miles from the New York primary food market. This metropolitan area supported about nine million people in 1919,[1] and its numbers have grown rapidly since then. The wide geographical range in the producing sections which supply the food for this metropolitan population gives national importance to the New York market; while consumers in all large urban communities have a like common interest in the economical distribution of their food supply. Producers and consumers are thus equally interested in reducing as far as possible the gap between producers' and consumers' prices.

Food producers are immediately interested in the prices received for their products at the farm, for the grower's money income depends upon prices at the point of origin. But it is the repeated purchases of many individual city consumers which are the ultimate source of farmers' incomes. Consumers therefore have an immediate interest in keeping city retail prices as close as possible to the prices received by producers; for it is the portion of the family income expended for food which determines the kind and quantity of

[1] *Report of Federal Trade Commission on Wholesale Marketing of Food*, June 30, 1919, p. 197.

nourishment secured. "Food absorbs 38.2 of the average American household's income. It therefore constitutes no inconsiderable part of the wage and salary cost in all production. Of two communities whose products enter the same market otherwise equally, that one which supplies its working people with food at a lower community cost either will pay its workers a higher real wage or will have a marked advantage in underselling the other through lower production costs. Both results may in some measure follow."[1] Careful consideration should therefore be given to factors in the methods of food handling which may influence the size of this price gap.

SIGNIFICANCE TO CONSUMERS

Authorities on diet hold that a substantial quantity of fresh fruits and vegetables in the daily menu is necessary to maintain health and efficiency. These articles are particularly rich in mineral salts and vitamines, and they supply the human system with important elements that are lacking in other foods. An adequate and well-distributed supply of fruits and vegetables is thus essential to the general well-being of the population.

Studies made by the United States Bureau of Labor Statistics[2] show that, while the average total quantity of food consumed per man per day in 1919 was slightly greater in New York City than in five other large urban areas in different sections of the United States, the daily consumption of fresh fruits and vegetables in the average dietary was materially lower in New York City, both in proportion to the total food purchased and in actual quantity. While in the St. Louis and Minneapolis areas these articles comprised

[1] *Ibid.*, p. 13.

[2] *Monthly Labor Review*, vol. ix, no. 2 (August, 1919), "A Study of Food Costs in Various Cities," by Prof. William F. Ogburn, pp. 1-25.

about 40 per cent, and in Boston 31 per cent, of all foods consumed, they were only 25 per cent of the total daily food consumption in New York. The individual consumption of perishables in other cities exceeded that in New York by from 21 per cent in Boston to 49 per cent in Minneapolis and St. Paul. The total quantity of food consumed per man per day in each of the six cities, the amount of fruits and vegetables, and the ratios of the latter to the total consumption in each respective city and to the fruit and vegetable consumption in New York, are shown in Table 1.

TABLE 1 [1]

DAILY FOOD CONSUMPTION PER PERSON [2] IN SIX LARGE CITIES

Locality	Total food	Fruits and vegetables		
		Amount consumed	Percentage of total food	Percentage of New York total
	Pounds	*Pounds*	*Per cent*	*Per cent*
New York	4.411	1.125	26.	100
Boston	4.345	1.362	31.	121
San Francisco	4.352	1.492	34.	133
Chicago	4.345	1.526	35.	136
St. Louis & E. St. Louis.	3.908	1.559	40.	138
Minneapolis & St. Paul..	4.287	1.676	39.	149

The studies referred to show also that the average cost of a standard dietary was considerably greater in New York than in any of the other cities. The annual cost of food for a standard working-class family in New York City was $50

[1] *Monthly Labor Review*, U. S. Bureau of Labor Statistics, August, 1919.

[2] Actual consumption of food yielding approximately 3500 calories per man per day, in standard working-class families consisting of husband, wife and 3 children, aged 2, 5 and 11 years, with total annual expenditure of $1300.

greater than in Boston, $65 more than in Chicago, $73 greater than in San Francisco, over $100 above that in St. Louis, and nearly $200 in excess of the annual family cost of food in the Twin Cities. The outlay in these other cities was from 7 per cent to 30 per cent below the average for families in New York. Table 2 gives the cost of adequate standard dietaries in each city, and the percentage reduction of each below the New York expenditures.

TABLE 2

COST OF ADEQUATE DIETARIES[1] IN SIX LARGE CITIES

Locality	Per man per day	Per family per year	Below New York outlay
	Cents	*Dollars*	*Per cent*
New York	57.6	678.73	..
Boston	53.4	628.92	7
Chicago	51,2	613.10	10
San Francisco	51.1	605.40	11
St. Louis & E. St. Louis	49.3	567.37	16
Minneapolis & St. Paul	42.6	485.29	29

From the data in these two tables, the consumption of fruits and vegetables appears to be closely related to the total monetary expenditure for food. As the outlay for food increases in the different cities the consumption of perishables diminishes. Since the expense of city distribution of fruits and vegetables is considerably greater than that for the more staple foods,[2] the higher cost of food to New York consumers indicates that they pay an even greater excess for these perishable articles, and in consequence of the high cost the quantity of them consumed is materially

[1] Actual consumption of food yielding approximately 3500 calories per man per day, in standard working-class families consisting of husband, wife and 3 children aged 2, 5 and 11 years, with total annual expenditure of $1300.

[2] See figures from various studies on pp. 50-52.

diminished. Reduction in the expense of distribution should therefore be a stimulus to increased consumption. To the nine million consumers whose food supply depends upon the metropolitan distribution system, this study of factors affecting the expense of city distribution is therefore of particular significance. "The whole industrial efficiency of the city is involved in this question of cheap food; and because New York is the great Atlantic gateway of the country, the problem of the efficient feeding of New York City widens to a national problem."[1]

SIGNIFICANCE TO FOOD PRODUCERS

The fresh fruits and vegetables which are consumed annually in the New York area are estimated to have a value at wholesale exceeding two hundred million dollars. In 1923 over 180,000 carloads of these products were shipped or trucked into the metropolitan area for local consumption. An average of five hundred carloads, worth from a half million to a million dollars, passes into and is sold in the New York market each day of the year.

Not more than ten per cent of this merchandise is locally grown, and only a scant five per cent is sold directly from farmer to retailer.[2] Ninety per cent of the total is shipped from producing areas that are from 30 miles to over 3,000 miles distant. Over one-half of the rail and water arrivals are transported five hundred miles or more. The bordering and nearby states of New York, New Jersey, Pennsylvania, Delaware, Maryland and the New England States produce only about 30 per cent of the total. Over one-fourth comes from the Pacific Coast, California alone supplying upwards of 20 per cent. One-sixth of the total is provided by up-

[1] *Report of Federal Trade Commission on Wholesale Maketing of Food*, p. 233.

[2] *Ibid.*, p. 218.

state New York, and Florida supplies one-seventh of the annual volume. Other important supply states are Virginia, North and South Carolina, Georgia and Texas. From various foreign countries come special articles,—early

TABLE 3

PRINCIPAL SOURCES OF FRESH FRUITS AND VEGETABLES, NEW YORK WHOLESALE MARKET, CALENDAR YEAR 1923

Source	Quantity	Percentage of total rail and water receipts (excluding bananas)
	Carloads	*Per cent*
California	30,665	21.5
New York	23,557	16.5
Florida	20,034	14.1
Virginia	9,425	6.6
New Jersey	8,517	6.0
Maine	6,541	4.6
South Carolina	5,756	4.0
Washington	5,394	3.8
North Carolina	3,967	2.8
Georgia	2,965	2.1
Oregon	2,703	1.9
Maryland	2,628	1.8
Texas	1,320	.9
All other domestic	9,674	1.8
Foreign	9,204	6.5
Small commodities not reported above	7,662	5.1
Total rail and water receipts	150,012[1]	100.0
Local truck-hauled produce (estimated)	19,000	
Bananas imported from Central and South America	13,500	
Total fresh fruits and vegetables from all sources	182,512	

tomatoes and melons from northern Mexico, fruits from Argentina, Chile, Italy and South Africa, cabbage from Germany and Holland, onions from Spain and Egypt,

[1] From *Market News Circular*, issued by U. S. Dept. of Agr. for New York Wholesale Market, February 15, 1924.

bananas from Central and South America. Because of the diversity and distance of sources, the average length of haul for all perishables consumed in the New York market in 1923 was upwards of 1,500 miles. The principal sources which supply the New York market, and the quantity and proportion contributed by each state are given in Table 3. This metropolitan consuming area is of as vital concern to truck-farmers and fruit-growers on the Pacific Coast and in the southern states as it is to nearby sections in the east. Efficient distribution in this area is thus a subject of national importance to food producers.

CHAPTER II

Metropolitan Distribution Agencies

WHOLESALE MARKET

Most of the fresh fruits and vegetables for the entire metropolitan area are distributed from a limited and highly centralized wholesale district which occupies about a half-mile of waterfront and adjacent streets along the lower west side of Manhattan Island. The perishable food for nine million consumers passes chiefly through this primary wholesale market. A small portion of the rail receipts is shipped over the New York Central Railroad directly to its Thirty-third Street yard. Minor portions are received also at the New Haven yards bordering the Harlem River in the Bronx, at the Pennsylvania yard in Newark, and at the Long Island Railroad terminals in Brooklyn. Very little local produce comes into the wholesale market from farms within trucking distance of New York, as this is hauled directly to the regional jobbing markets. With the minor exceptions stated, the whole supply of fresh fruits and vegetables passes through the wholesale market.

"Through this market must be distributed in the course of nine hours of each day some 40 or 50 commodities representing in their grades upwards of a hundred items of traffic. Few of them are constant for long periods, so that in the course of a season a great many more than a hundred items of traffic are handled. The volume of trade in (all) perishable produce on the New York market is enormous, said to be upwards of seven hundred million dollars a year. The greater part of it falls within four months of the year. Through this market must be negotiated all the irregularities of growing conditions of highly perishable crops that must be rushed at express speed to reach the market under normal conditions, and must not be delayed in distribution when they reach the market itself." [1]

From the central wholesale market the supply for the different sections of the metropolitan area has to be hauled to the points of secondary distribution by motor-truck or team. There are no railroad facilities whereby any portion of it may be transported to local distribution points. In consequence of the congestion and heavy hauling charges which attend this addition to street traffic, the expense of distributing goods from the primary market is materially increased.

Jobbing Markets

There are five jobbing markets through which food supplies pass on their way to different parts of the metropolitan area. These are the secondary channels through which the carlot receipts of the wholesale market are distributed by jobbers to retailers after being split up into smaller sized lots convenient for retail trade. The largest of these jobbing markets is in downtown New York, adjacent to the wholesale section. It extends for several blocks along Washington Street and intersecting streets. This is the principal source of supply for most retailers of Manhattan Island south of Fifty-ninth Street. Stores in Jersey City and other municipalities near the western waterfront in New Jersey also are supplied chiefly from this downtown jobbing market. Most retailers in the borough of Queens, and some in Brooklyn, as well as scattered dealers in upper New York and the

[1] *Report of Federal Trade Commission on Wholesale Marketing of Food*, p. 217.

Bronx, come here for perishable goods, being attracted to the downtown market by the more extensive supplies available because of its proximity to the primary market.

There are two other jobbing markets on Manhattan Island which supply retailers in their respective vicinities. West of Tenth Avenue and below Fourteenth Street is the Gansevoort Market, which is the principal source for the large hotels and restaurants. On the northeast corner of the Island is the Harlem Market extending from 100th Street to 106th Street along the East River. From this center are supplied most of the retail trade north of Fifty-ninth Street and that of the Bronx. The Borough of Brooklyn, and a part of Queens is supplied from the Wallabout jobbing market, which is adjacent to the Brooklyn Navy Yard on the East River. The remaining secondary market of the metropolitan area is in the heart of Newark, New Jersey. Most of the retailers of that city and surrounding communities secure provisions there.

In each of the jobbing markets, excepting that in downtown New York, there is a farmer's market, with a reserved open plaza, where locally-grown produce is hauled and sold directly to retailers and jobbers by growers and local merchants.

The number and location of primary and secondary dealers in the wholesale and jobbing markets are given in Table 4. As frequent changes take place, with the establishment of new firms and the disappearance of old ones, these figures are only approximately accurate. With changing seasons the number fluctuates, increasing in the fall of the year and diminishing in winter and spring. There is also a considerable overlapping of wholesalers' and jobbers' functions, which makes exact classification difficult. Some wholesale receivers do a brokerage business, while some dealers have jobbing branches in the secondary markets in addition to their

TABLE 4

PRIMARY AND SECONDARY MARKETS, NEW YORK METROPOLITAN AREA, 1923

	Firms
Wholesale	
Wholesalers and large handlers	115
Auction brokers and growers' agents	135
Primary dealers	250
Jobbing	
Downtown N. Y. Market	150
Wallabout "	115
Harlem "	100
Gansevoort "	80
Newark "	50
Other miscellaneous	45
Out-of-town jobbers	90
Secondary dealers	630
Total wholesalers and jobbers	880

wholesale business. Many jobbers do a semi-retail business also. The total number of individuals and firms carrying on wholesale or jobbing business in fresh fruits and vegetables is estimated to vary roughly from 800 to 1,000. From one-fourth to one-third of these are wholesale dealers in the primary market. The manner in which goods are received and passed on through the wholesale and jobbing markets for distribution by retailers to metropolitan consumers, is illustrated graphically in Figure 1.

Retailers

A full account of the retailing agencies that serve consumers in the metropolitan area would include not only the local community stores, but also several other types of retail distribution which serve special classes of consumers. In volume of perishable goods sold, and in number of establishments, the grocery stores and specialized fruit and vegetable stores are most important. In the poorer sections of Greater New York there are over fifty retail pushcart markets, in

HOW THE NEW YORK DISTRICT RECEIVES AND DISTRIBUTES
ITS FRESH FRUIT AND VEGETABLE SUPPLY
250 WHOLESALERS
600 JOBBERS
RETAILERS
RAIL 85
C A R R I E R S
WATER 5
TRUCK 10
THE NEW YORK WHOLESALE MARKET — 90% OF ALL RECEIPTS
LOCAL PRODUCERS 10%
DOWN-TOWN N.Y. 150 FIRMS
WALLABOUT 115 FIRMS
HARLEM 100 FIRMS
GANSEVOORT 80 FIRMS
NEWARK 50 FIRMS
MISCELLANEOUS 135 FIRMS
10,000 GROCERY STORES (Greater N.Y.)
3,500 FRUIT-VEGETABLE STORES
7,000 PUSHCARTS
4,000 HUCKSTERS
HOTELS & RESTAURANTS
SIX MILLION CONSUMERS

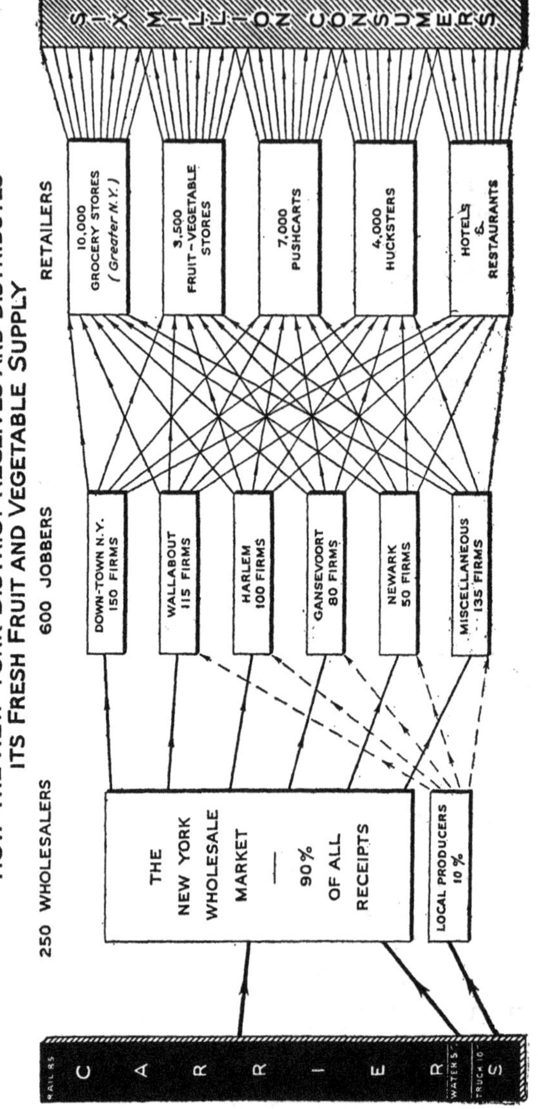

FIGURE I

which seven thousand street vendors sell fresh fruits and vegetables to the extent of about 35 million dollars a year.[1] Some four thousand itinerant hucksters' wagons also circulate periodically within the metropolitan area. These two types are the most elastic part of the retailing system, providing an outlet for great quantities of low-priced perishables.

The large transient and suburban population served by the many hotels and restaurants of New York gives importance to these agencies as outlets for a considerable volume of perishables. To them should be added also the hundreds of railway trains and steamships which are provisioned daily in New York for their outbound trips.

Among minor distribution agencies should be considered the roadside market-stands along the rural highways leading out from the metropolitan centers. While these are outlets mainly for seasonal locally-grown farm produce, some of them maintain a continuous trade through summer and fall, with the addition of shipped-in produce from the city. These roadside markets have assumed considerable mercantile importance in recent years since automobile travel has become so general. Receipts from them in several agricultural districts of New Jersey in 1924 were more than double those of the preceding year.[2] Recognition of their growing importance is evidenced in recent proposals to standardize them and place them under the supervision of the State Bureau of Markets.[3]

The miscellaneous retailing agencies just mentioned, including push carts, hucksters, hotels and restaurants, railway trains, steamships and farmers' roadside markets, are estimated to distribute from 20 per cent to 25 per cent of all

[1] U. S. Dept. of Agr. Preliminary Report, "Push Cart Markets in New York City," by Earl R. French, April, 1925, p. 2.

[2] *Press Circular of N. J. Dept. of Agr.*, Bureau of Markets, Oct. 26, 1924.

[3] *Circular of U. S. Dept. of Agr.*, "Marketing Activities," Apr. 15, 1925.

fresh fruits and vegetables consumed in the metropolitan area. The remaining amount, which comprises from 75 to 80 per cent of all receipts, is distributed through local community stores. Because the greater portion of metropolitan consumers make their individual purchases through these neighborhood retail stores, the present study is particularly concerned with their activities.

DIFFERENT TYPES OF STORES

Within the five boroughs of Greater New York there are upwards of 13,500 stores which retail fresh fruits and vegetables. Over one-half of these are independent grocery stores which carry perishables as an adjunct to their grocery business. Slightly over one-fourth of the total number are specialized retailers handling fruits and vegetables only. Chain grocery stores are one-fifth of the total. The number of each of these three types of retailers in each borough, and the totals for the whole city, are given in Table 5.

TABLE 5

RETAIL STORES IN BOROUGHS OF GREATER NEW YORK,[1] 1924

	Manhattan	*Brooklyn*	*Bronx*	*Queens*	*Richmond*	*Total*
Unit grocery	3215	3016	647	379	36	7293
Fruit-vegetable .	1159	1662	415	261	26	3523
Chain grocery ..	862	1952	392	380	69	2755
Total number ...	5236	5730	1454	1020	131	13571

These three types of retail stores vary materially in their importance as outlets for perishables because of wide variations both in volume of total business, and in the proportion of this which represents sales of fruits and vegetables. From inquiries among representative grocers, both independent and chain, the proportion of these articles sold by grocery

[1] Data furnished by New York University Bureau of Business Research.

stores is estimated to average about 20 per cent of their total trade. The business of fruit-vegetable stores, on the other hand, consists almost wholly of perishables. The apparently smaller size places of business of some fruit-vegetable dealers is considered to be offset by a more rapid stock-turn than that of grocery stores. Giving due consideration to the numerical importance of each store type, and to differences in the proportions of perishables which they handle, their relative importance as outlets for fruit and vegetables in greater New York is: Fruit-vegetable stores, 64 per cent, unit grocery stores, 26 per cent, chain grocery stores, 10 per cent. The specialized retailers are thus of primary importance in city distribution, accounting for nearly two-thirds of all fruits and vegetables sold through neighborhood stores. Independent unit grocery stores dispose of but one-fourth of the total, and chain grocery stores sell only one-tenth. These proportions are regarded as holding true throughout the metropolitan area.

Store Management

The prevailing form of management in the metropolitan area is that of the single retail unit, operated as an independent neighborhood store. Eighty per cent of the retailers who sell fruits and vegetables operate such independent units. Each unit is conducted by its own local proprietor, who determines its policy and fixes its selling prices according to his own judgment.

Of retail shops that sell fruits and vegetables, one-fifth are chain stores. These differ from the independent units in that each one is operated as a part of a unified system controlled by a central organization. Uniform policies and prices are thus established for all stores of a given chain system. There is a local manager for each store, in place of the independent proprietor. The manager conducts the business according to standardized methods of procedure, with limited local autonomy, according to a fixed plan of operation and a uniform scale of selling prices. Only such standard commodities are offered for sale as are in general community demand. Specialities that are sought only by a limited number of consumers are not usually carried. By thus limiting varieties and brands, chain stores carry a smaller supply of goods in stock, whose turnover is more rapid than that when a wider variety is maintained.

The centralized operation of chain stores gives them distinct advantages in purchasing supplies. Staple articles such as potatoes and apples are purchased in the wholesale market or at shipping points, by expert buyers who can take advantage of favorable conditions in the market. Supplies for the individual stores are loaded at the city receiving point or at the central warehouse into trucks for direct distribution to each store according to the requisition of its manager. In addition to the price advantages from large purchases, the chain system of direct distribution eliminates the expense of trucking to and from the jobbing market, as well as the loss of time required in selecting small individual lots for each store in the jobbing market. The chain store system can thus eliminate certain distribution expenses by large quantity buying and direct delivery of supplies from the primary market, and by its standardized procedure with the variety of goods restricted to articles of general community demand.

Specialization

Among retailers of perishable produce there are all degrees of specialization, from that of the general grocery store which adds potatoes and oranges to its main line of groceries, to the shops which sell nothing but fruits and vegetables. The line of specialization is therefore not clearly marked. Nearly all grocery stores carry the less perishable staples, such as potatoes, oranges and onions. Many of them carry also seasonal articles that are in regular demand, such as lettuce, spinach, and apples. The larger higher-class grocery stores sell a fuller line of perishables, including the principal specialty articles. Some stores carry a full line of fruits and vegetables and only a limited line of groceries, such as canned goods or coffee and dairy products. The widest variety of perishables is carried by the larger specialized fruit and vegetable stores. Some of these sell only fruits, and others sell only vegetables, but most of them handle both.

Preferences of consumers to do all of the daily shopping for family provisions in one store seems to have been the basic inducement for the addition by chain stores of fruits and vegetables to their original lines of general groceries. It is stated that the original purpose in adding perishables was to attract and hold grocery customers, rather than to make a direct profit from the added articles. These were employed to draw trade to the more profitable highly-priced groceries. Some of the chain systems use potatoes in this way frankly as a leader, selling them at prices that yield little or no profit. While the majority of chain stores sell only the more staple fruits and vegetables, the tendency in many of them is to increase the variety of perishables so as to include all seasonal articles whose demand is general enough to assure a profit.

Classes of Retail Trade

There is marked divergence in the classes of retail trade in different parts of the Metropolitan Area. Gradation from an exclusive high-class residence section with luxurious apartments to one occupied by the poorer working classes is often found within a range of but two or three city blocks. The intermingling of such diverse areas is attended by wide diversity in the class of trade. Variability in tastes and in purchasing power increases the diversity of food articles that are required by different consumers. Shops carrying only the highest qualities of goods for an exclusive trade are often located in close proximity to those carrying the cheaper goods for a more modest trade. Stores which attempt to serve both classes must carry a variety of extra-quality goods for wealthy residents and the standard brands for the others.

Retailers catering to the higher-class trade sell the widest variety of high-quality goods, and render the maximum of service. Their stores have wide frontage with spacious interiors, requiring high rentals. In the poorer neighborhoods where lower rents prevail the low-price stores predominate. They carry a restricted variety of staples and the cheaper grades of seasonal commodities. The stores are usually small, with narrow frontage, oftentimes occupying but one-half the space and frontage of a standard sized store. These low-price retailers render the minimum of service, grant little or no credit and make few or no deliveries. The most numerous retailers are those operating stores whose trade is with the great body of middle-class families of moderate incomes. The characteristics of this trade are standard qualities and a considerable variety of staple and seasonable commodities, with moderate prices. Limited credit is granted to regular customers, with limited delivery service. There are also numerous large general stores whose business is extensive enough to include both a high-class clientele and the medium and low-price trade. These maintain the most extensive stocks of goods, and the largest personel. For the exacting high-class clientele they carry fancy specialty goods, while they keep also an extensive stock of standard articles to supply the low-price trade. Large-scale operation enables these general stores to sell the widest range of commodities and to keep the fullest supply of fresh goods.

Size and Equipment of Stores

The size of business is, of course, highly variable, ranging all the way from that of a small fruit store whose proprietor is the sole attendant, to the large establishment with as many as eight to ten employees. The most numerous type of retail store, both grocery and fruit-vegetable, has a staff of two persons, a store frontage of 12 to 18 feet, and a depth of 20 to 30 feet. The staff consists of the proprietor and an employed helper, husband and wife, or a dual working partnership. Many stores are operated as family enterprises, in which the parents or father and son or daughter provide the attention and labor. The proportion of larger stores with eight to ten employees is not great, but the total volume of their business is much greater than their proportionate number. In these larger stores there is usually one person who keeps accounts, and another to make deliveries. The smaller stores which deliver often hire a boy or a man on a part-time basis for this purpose.

Store frontages vary from narrow shops that are little more than stalls, not exceeding 6 or 8 feet in width, to double fronts of 24 to 30 feet. The most common size of frontage is 12 to 15 feet. It tends to be narrower in the higher rent districts. Where a grocery store handles fruits and vegetables, the full frontage is generally used for displaying perishables. The depth varies all the way from 10 feet to 40 feet. The rear part of the store is generally used as a temporary storage for supplies. A few stores have cellars which are used for this purpose, but their number is limited. Most retailers have a desk or an office in the rear end of the store for the keeping of business records; but many of the smaller ones use only the drawer of a cash register for this purpose. Chain stores frequently occupy but one-half of the frontage and space of a divided store, thereby cutting down the item of rent. Fruit and vegetable retailers often use half of a store in a similar way.

The equipment outside the store is that required for bringing in supplies from the jobbing market, and for delivery to customers where this service is rendered. The smaller stores have no inward delivery facilities, finding it cheaper to hire delivery or to buy from small jobbers who deliver to their store without charge. Many of the larger stores maintain a horse and wagon or a medium-size auto truck for bringing their supplies from market, using the same vehicle for delivering sales to customers. Most retailers prefer the automobile to the horse and wagon. Some of them, however, hold that the horse and wagon is more economical, because it requires less high-priced labor to operate.

The trading area of the retail store varies according to location and size of business. The radius of stores in the congested residence sections often does not extend more than two or three blocks distant, and in many cases it is less than that.

EVOLUTION OF PRESENT DISTRIBUTION SYSTEM

In the days when New York was a thriving small city, its supplies of fresh produce were grown on nearby farms and were sold in the local market by the growers directly to the householders. The family market-basket and the regular trip to the city-owned farmers' market were then established institutions. " Relative to their actual needs and standards of life, the early New Yorkers and their markets were more ' modern ' than they have been since. New York City was well served when all its perishable food came from the neighboring farms. Much of it was brought by barge, and the early market places were at the water side. In Revolutionary days there were four such markets along the shore line, with one interior market on Broadway. The markets that followed were mostly at interior points, but they remained distinctly market-basket markets, supplied from the farms of the country-side. By 1838 there were 13 such city markets. The farm-wagon markets which attach to the Wallabout, the West Washington and Harlem Markets, are relics of the early marketing system when the country-side from a radius of 30 miles supplied the city entirely." [1]

With the growth of population and the need for production from distant points to meet the city's increased food requirements, changes came about in the whole scheme of distribution. Rapid long-distance shipment of perishables, made possible by the extension of railroad transportation and the use of refrigerator cars, rendered the earlier system of local markets entirely inadequate. A complete change thus took place in the distribution of farm produce, in which commission merchants and jobbers gradually came into the market as intermediaries. With the introduction of the wholesaling principle, the function of provisioning the family, which was performed earlier through the local farmers' markets, was taken over by neighborhood retail stores. "The corner grocery and produce stores have now superseded the housewives' market-basket of the early day in the habits of New Yorkers. So it has come about that the public market-places originally designed for other purposes have gradually integrated with a scheme for distribution based upon deliveries at the rail and water terminals of the public carriers, with a distribution effected through an elaborate machinery of wholesalers, jobbers and retailers." [1] The geographic location of present wholesale and jobbing markets and the channels of distribution to retail

[1] *Report of Federal Trade Commission*, p. 204.

[1] *Ibid.*, p. 205.

DISTRIBUTION OF FRESH FRUITS
AND VEGETABLES
New York Metropolitan Area
Passaic
10 Miles
From Primary Market
Bronx
Manhattan
Newark
Jersey
City
N
G
H
P
W
Elizabeth
Bayonne
Brooklyn
STATEN
ISLAND
Primary Wholesale Market
Jobbing Markets: (W, Wallabout, Brooklyn; G, Gansevoort, Manhattan;
H. Harlem, Manhattan, N. Newark, N.J.)
Retail stores included in this study

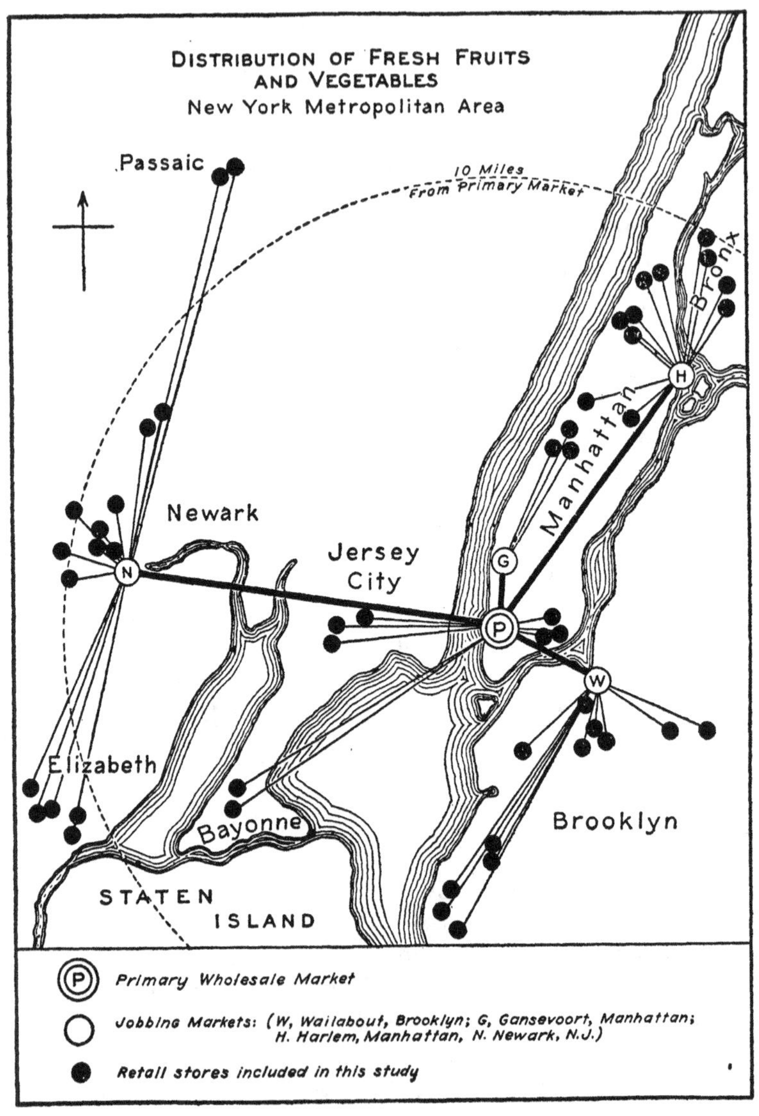

FIGURE 2

stores in various parts of the metropolitan area, are indicated in Figure 2.

The advent of modern apartment houses and large tenements with their restricted space and lack of facilities for keeping provisions, have forced radical changes in the food-purchasing habits of consumers. The household now seldom carries any stock of family provisions, but makes food purchases from day to day at the nearby retail store, with no need to look forward and plan its requirements in advance. The neighborhood store has replaced the pantry and provision cellar of earlier days. The retailer keeps a small stock of provisions on hand, and replenishes his supply from the current market arrivals, which provide a fresh and continuous stream of goods assembled from near and far. These changes in supply and in the methods of distribution bring conveniences and services to the consumer that were undreamed of by the housewife of former periods. "There has grown up the neighborhood grocery store to do for the housewife what she has gradually ceased to do for herself, namely, to buy and bring into the neighborhood, to select and assort, and invitingly exhibit the receipts of the general market in such a way as to suggest and facilitate the daily home menu. The delicatessen store carries the process yet a stage further and serves partially prepared food; while the wagon and pushcart peddler wheels his assorted supply under the flat dweller's window. Along with the goods which he delivers, the neighborhood grocery man or delicatessen man has come to perform a very large personal service in this way; and he furthermore holds himself ready to perform this personal service during any hour of the day or night that his store is open, and to deliver in any irregular quantity that the passing whim of the housekeeper who has not planned ahead may impose upon him."[1] Any fair

[1] *Ibid.*, p. 217.

evaluation of the present methods of food distribution must take account of the important place of personal service in consumers' purchases. "This sale of personal service along with the commodity is the striking phase of the New York produce distribution. It is a large item in the high cost of the produce sold. It is true the vagaries of the ultimate consumer are not directly handled by the wholesaler and jobber, but they are among the ultimate factors with which they must reckon, and for which they must provide by assorting and packing and searching out the markets for their particular goods."

RETAILERS' GENERAL FUNCTIONS

The retailer's important place in the distribution system is due to several essential functions which he performs for the community. The title of "consumer's purchasing agent" aptly characterises his role as an agency for meeting the individual requirements of the consuming public. In filling this role, he performs various services that are an inseparable part of the system of distribution as constituted at present. These services take form in a variety of distinct activities that may be grouped in the following manner:

Assembling in one conveniently accessible place a variety of different commodities required by his trade.

Maintaining at all times a fresh daily supply of the articles available in the market.

Breaking up the shipping package or jobbers' unit into small-quantity units convenient for consumers' individual requirements.

Selecting, grading and arranging his goods for retail sale.

Displaying his stock for inspection and selection by customers.

Measuring, weighing or counting each sale, putting it up in a convenient package for delivery, computing its value, and securing payment from the customer.

Assembling a Conveniently Accessible Variety of Goods

The diverse preferences of consumers for variety in their food require retailers to maintain a wide range of articles to satisfy various classes of trade. The demands of customers has much to do in determining the extent of the line of goods offered for sale. Frequent experimentation shows the extent of the demand for particular products. Competition may lead dealers to carry articles that bring little or no profit, in order to hold trade which might otherwise drift away to other dealers. Addition of new articles to a line of goods tends to reduce the volume of sale of the others; and each increase in the number of individual items carried in stock increases the risk of loss through incorrect estimate of the quantity of each which can be disposed of promptly. In consequence of the wide variety maintained, purchases in the jobbing market must be made in numerous small quantities extending over a wide range of articles.

The extent to which retailers render service by bringing together in their community a variety of products from widely separated regions, is well illustrated in Table 6. This list contains 32 varieties of fruits and 40 kinds of vegetables, assembled in one grocery store for a single day's business. They are products of widely divergent sources, some of them as distant as California, Central American and Spain. Each variety was purchased in the jobbing market in a separate package or in bulk, in quantity sufficient to satisfy a number of individual customers' wants. Although the range of commodities and varieties in the example given is greater than that maintained by the majority of retailers, it would probably be exceeded in numerous stores at the height of the season.

TABLE 6

VARIETIES DISPLAYED FOR SALE BY A MANHATTAN GROCERY STORE, WEDNESDAY, OCTOBER 22, 1924

Fruits

Variety	*Source*
Banana apples	Pacific Coast
Delicious apples	Pacific Coast
Jonathan apples (2 sizes)	Pacific Coast
Greening apples	New York State
Twenty-ounce apples	New York State
Red bananas	Central America
Yellow bananas	Central America
Crabapples	New York State
Cranberries	Massachusetts
Concord grapes	New York State
Delaware grapes	New York State
Niagara grapes	New York State
Camille grapes	California
Malaga grapes	California
Seedless grapes	California
Grapefruit (3 sizes)	Florida
Huckleberries	New York State
Lemons	California
Casaba melons	California
Honey Dew melons	California
Oranges (2 brands)	California
Peaches (2 grades)	New Jersey
Raspberries	New York
Alligator pears	California
Bartlett pears	California
Bartlett pears	New York State
Bosc pears	California
Comice pears	California
Seckel pears	California
Seckel pears	New York State
Persimmons	Southern States
Blue plums	New York State
Yellow plums	New York State
Quinces	California

Vegetables

Artichokes	California
Beets	Local
Brussels sprouts	Local
White cabbage	New York State
Red cabbage	New York State
Savoy cabbage	New York State
Cantaloupes	Colorado
Carrots	New York State
Cauliflower	New York State
Celery	New York State
Celeriac	New York State
Chickory	Long Island
Sweet corn	New Jersey
Cucumbers	New York State
Egg plant	New York State
Kohl rabi	New York State
Boston lettuce	New York State
Lima beans	New York State
Green onions	Local
Silver skin onions	New York State
Spanish onions	Spain
Yellow onions	New York State
White potatoes	Long Island
Parsley	Local
Green peas	Local
Red radishes	Local
White radishes	Local
Rutabagas	Local
Salsify	Local
Spinach	Local
Green string beans	Local
Yellow string beans	Local
Sweet potatoes	New Jersey
Tomatoes	New Jersey
White turnips	Local
Water cress	Local

Maintenance of Continuous Supplies

To maintain a stock of perishable goods in attractive salable condition, the retailer has to replenish it frequently with repeated small additions. He must therefore buy goods daily in summer, and at least two or three times a week in cool weather. He cannot take advantage of heavy market receipts to stock up against price advances, but must estimate carefully the requirements of his trade from day to day. The demand for a wide range of articles, the diverse qualities and grades of goods available in the market, and the necessity of keeping his stock in fresh condition, thus combine to force the retailer to make frequent purchases in the jobbing market, in relatively small quantities.

Breaking up Shipping Package into Consumers' Sale Units

Fresh fruits and vegetables are bought and sold in the New York wholesale and jobbing markets mainly in the original shipping packages,—in crates, boxes, barrels, baskets, sacks, or in bulk by the hundred-weight or hundred-count. Retail sales are made in small quantities, in terms of a few pounds or quarts, by the dozen, or by single count. To dispose of a single retailer's package or a hundred-weight in this way requires from fifteen to fifty separate transactions. Although a limited number of consumers buy their supplies in considerably larger quantities, this small size retailing is the prevailing practice throughout Greater New York. In the surrounding smaller cities and suburban centers the proportion of larger size sales is somewhat greater.

The extent of breaking up involved in retail distribution may be illustrated by the manner in which a carload of lettuce is subdivided. There are approximately 320 crates in a carload of New York State lettuce, and each crate contains two dozen heads. The ordinary sale to a jobber is twenty crates; thus sixteen sales are made in the wholesale market to dispose of a carload to the jobbers. The prevailing sale to retailers is a single crate. To distribute the carload into the hands of retailers thus requires 320 transactions by jobbers. When the housewife buys a single head of lettuce she purchases one twenty-fourth of a crate. If each retail sale consisted of a single head, the retailer would thus have to make twenty-four transactions to dispose of a single crate of lettuce. To distribute a whole carload to consumers in single-head sales would thus require 7,680 retail transactions.

In the break-up of a package into small units of sale, some loss in volume is almost inevitable. With many commodities exactness in weighing or measuring is difficult to attain, and any slight error is expected to be in the customer's favor. There is thus a considerable element of shrinkage in retailing, due to the division of a package or gross quantity into numerous small units.

There is another source of loss, arising from portions of packages remaining unsold. Frequently a retailer has an insistent but limited demand for a particular article, so that he finds it difficult to dispose of an entire package. To carry it on hand at all he must ordinarily buy an unbroken package from the jobber, with the prospect of having part of it unsold on his hands. In one such instance a grocer sold five quinces to a valued regular customer, charging ten cents apiece for them. To the customer's protest against what was considered an exorbitant charge, the retailer explained that he had had to buy a whole bushel of quinces in the market to fill the one order, and that there was so slight a call for them from his regular trade that it was doubtful if he could sell the rest of the bushel at all.

Assorting and Arranging Goods for Sale

In retailing perishables, a considerable amount of time and labor is required to prepare goods for sale and to keep them in salable condition after they arrive at the retail store. Carefully packed and graded articles such as oranges and boxed apples may require simply the removal of their paper wrappings. But even the most rigidly packed goods deteriorate to some degree in storage or in shipping, so that when opened for sale the package may contain defective specimens. With careless grading and packing inferior articles may be included, which make it necessary to re-sort the package into proper grades or sizes for retail sale. The work of putting goods into salable condition is generally done after they are received at the store, although a small proportion of jobbers recondition and repack their merchandise and guarantee its quality.

Leafy vegetables such as lettuce, cabbage and celery become soiled or withered through handling or exposure in shipment, so that the outer leaves must be removed. Root vegetables are often dirty, so that they require cleaning at the store. Some articles require a moist atmosphere to maintain crispness, and these must be kept sprinkled with cold water or enclosed in a cool chamber.

The insistence of consumers upon the privilege of sorting over a retailer's stock to select their purchases is an important item in increasing distribution expense. In making their selections, prospective customers frequently handle goods and leave the rejected articles soiled or disarranged. After a display has been handled by several customers, its attractive appearance is lost and its salability is thus impaired. Illustrative of this, a critical consumer of a high-class store selected three ears of sweet corn out of a dozen and discarded the other nine after opening their husks, because the kernels were not filled out to the extreme tip of the cob. With this mark of handling, the rejected ears could be sold to other customers only at a reduction in price, although they were sound and of good quality. The first customer's objection to the high charge for three ears of corn sorted out of an entire dozen, in comparison with the per-dozen quotation for standard goods in the wholesale market, overlooked entirely the loss which the retailer must bear on rejected goods because he grants the privilege of selection.

Display for Inspection

Display of the retailers' wares for the observation and inspection of customers is so general a practice that it is hardly thought of as a distinct function of distribution. Yet this is a real service which requires much effort on the part of the retailer. Consumers insist upon seeing the goods offered for sale, so that they may inspect them before purchasing. In recognition of this preference, retailers generally display

FIGURE 3

their stocks as freely and as attractively as possible. A large proportion of the goods they sell are first transferred from containers and arranged upon benches or racks or counters, where they will be easily accessible to customers. This arrangement of goods requires quite an outlay of time and labor, in addition to the store space which they occupy. A typical display of fruits and vegetables in front of a Manhattan store is shown in Figure 3.

MAKING THE SALE

The services heretofore described are all performed in anticipation of consumers' requirements, and in advance of sale. They are preliminary to the retailer's immediate purpose, which is to make individual sales of his goods in the kind and quantity desired by his customers. Filling a customer's order involves a number of separate acts, viz: (a) taking from the display space or from the reserve stock the goods desired by the customer, (b) weighing or measuring or counting the desired quantity, (c) putting this up in a satisfactory package for delivery to customer, (d) computing the amount of the sale, (e) making a record of the transaction, and (f) obtaining payment. These final acts in completing a retail transaction are preceded by a number of preparatory steps on the part of the retailer. Each sale is a matter of individual personal attention. Each of these separate acts has to be repeated to fill each customer's order. They are performed millions of times a year by the retailers who supply metropolitan consumers with their daily food.

PHYSICAL LOSSES IN RETAIL SELLING

Losses in physical volume occur in the handling of perishables to a much greater extent than with more highly standardized non-perishable goods. The wide variability in qualities produced in different seasons and different shipping areas, and variation in grading and packing for market, make it difficult to avoid a considerable loss from these causes. Despite the improvement that has been made in market standardization, the diversity of conditions of production and shipping prevents the general application of rigid standards such as are possible with non-perishables. A favorable season with abundant high-quality goods may be followed by one of limited supplies and inferior qualities. Weather conditions in the period between packing of goods and delivery to consumers, also, have much to do with the condition of fruits and vegetables when finally offered for consumption.

Physical losses in retailing arise from several sources. One of these is the shrinkage in volume accompanying the regrading and reconditioning of articles when removed from the original package for sale. For example, in hampers of lettuce and in barrels of apples inferior specimens are often found, which can be sold only at reduced prices, or may have to be discarded entirely. Specimens of cantaloupes are frequently bruised in shipment so that decay sets in. Re-selection for retail sale thus entails considerable loss in volume.

Loss in volume also takes place from shrinkage in actual contents of the original shipping package. Goods which evaporate quickly lose considerable weight between the time of packing and the time of retailing. A barrel of spinach, for example, whose contents normally weigh about 35 pounds, may vary in weight 10 or 15 pounds.

With highly perishable commodities, too, occasional losses are hard to avoid from non-sale of sound goods, because of the retailer's inability to gauge accurately the consumer demand at a particular time. Even with drastic reductions in price, goods frequently remain unsold until so deteriorated that they have to be thrown away, thus entailing a total loss to the community. Skill of the retailer in making his purchases is necessary to prevent considerable loss from this source, especially in warm weather.

In the absence of quantitative studies of the physical losses incurred by American retailers from these sources, one can only hazard a rough guess as to their average amount. An extensive inquiry in 1923 by the British Ministry of Agriculture,[1] into the expense of distributing fresh fruits and

[1] *Interim Report on Fruits and Vegetables*, by Departmental Committee on Distribution and Prices of Agricultural Produce, 1923, p. 63.

vegetables in English towns and cities, indicated that the average losses in volume in retailing had a range from 8½ per cent to 19 per cent, classified under the following four headings:

	Loss in volume
Reselection: sorting, grading and marking down for deterioration	2¾ per cent to 5 per cent
Losses in retail weighing and measuring	2¾ " to 4¾ "
Short weight or count in original packages	½ " to 5 "
Unsold goods	2½ " to 4¼ "
Total physical losses	8½ per cent to 19 per cent

The lower figures are for cooperative stores, while the higher ones are for private retailers. Assuming similar conditions to exist in American retailing, it seems probable that the physical loss in selling perishables through retail stores is generally in excess of ten per cent of their original volumes.

RETAIL PRICE POLICIES

A canvass of typical metropolitan stores indicated that among independent retailers no uniform or systematic plan is adhered to in fixing their selling prices. Past experience and the practices of competitors appear to be the principal guides. Some high-class retailers, however, whose stores are conducted on strict business principles, have a consistent policy of adding to the cost of their goods a definite percentage which is considered necessary to cover retailing expenses.

A number of retailers who were personally interviewed stated that changes in their selling prices were made according to changes in the actual cost of their new supplies, and not in conformity with general changes in market quotations. This indicates that some retailers advance their selling prices to coincide with the actual increase in outlay, rather than simply to parallel current market variations. Consequently a lag exists between wholesale and retail prices, whose interval represents the time required to dispose of the retailer's usual stock on hand.

Price reductions appear to operate in a similar way, although competition tends to force retailers to bring their prices into line with those of other stores which have purchased new supplies at lower cost. Competition is thus a dominant influence in bringing about price uniformity, tending to hold the prices of competing retailers in a locality close together. The higher-class merchants feel competition less keenly than do the middle-class and low-price stores, because the former have a greater measure of local monopoly in the sale of guaranteed high-quality goods. Not only is it true that the usual supply of such goods is so limited that they do not come into competition with the general market supply, but the customers of high-class stores are probably less sensitive to price changes.

Sharp price changes have disadvantages to consumers as well as to retailers. The public becomes accustomed to an established price, and is disturbed by sudden changes. Consumers seem to buy according to habit rather than from conscious motives of economy. Retail prices are therefore relatively much more stable from week to week than are wholesale prices. Rather than to attempt adjustment of prices to accord with slight market changes, retailers find it more satisfactory to maintain fairly steady prices at levels which will cover the ups and downs of the market. Retail price variations for different qualities and varieties, are much less marked, also, than are these variations in the wholesale market.

GENERAL EXPENSE OF DISTRIBUTION

The incompleteness of retailers' sale records, and the lack of detailed statistical studies in this field, make it difficult to obtain anything more than general statements of approximate retailing expense. Such studies as have been made have dealt for the most part with general groceries, or with particular single commodities such as bread, meat, and milk. The Joint Commission of Agricultural Inquiry, appointed by the 67th Congress of the United States, conducted extensive studies in 1921 into the marketing and distribution of foods and other articles. Surveys of the distribution of perishable farm products in Metropolitan Boston have also been made by the Massachusetts Department of Agriculture, in cooperation with the United States Department of Agriculture. A survey of the sale of perishable goods in the Center Market of Washington, D. C., was conducted in 1923 under the direct supervision of the United States Department of Agriculture. A number of other studies into the retailing of particular articles have been made in the last few years by the same agency. In England, also, an extensive survey of the marketing of fruits and vegetables was conducted in 1923 by the British Ministry of Agriculture.

Analysis of the operating expenses of grocery stores have been made by several agencies. The Federal Food Board and the New York State Food Commission in 1917 made a wartime study of prices in representative grocery stores and meat stores in Greater New York. The most comprehensive and detailed studies in this field are those by the Harvard Bureau of Business Research, which are based upon financial statements from a large number of retailers in different towns and cities of the United States and Canada. The University of Wisconsin, the University of Nebraska, and the University of Oregon have conducted more limited similar studies.

Although the studies by various agencies are too greatly diversified in scope, duration, and method of analysis to justify detailed comparisons, it is instructive to observe their general results. A summary of these studies and of such others as have come to the writer's attention, is therefore presented in Table 7. This gives the agency making each of the respective studies, the scope of the inquiry, and the approximate average retailing expense, expressed as a percentage of total receipts from sales. This percentage margin thus indicates the portion of the consumers' outlays which was required to cover the retailing services. The footnotes indicate the publications or manuscripts in which details of the respective studies are set forth more fully.

The various studies show a range in the proportion of retailers' receipts absorbed in the distribution process from a minimum of 14 per cent to a maximum of 61 per cent. The margin for fruits and vegetables is seen generally to be noticeably higher than that for other food articles. These perishables have a range in eleven independent studies from 20 per cent to 61 per cent, while the range in nine studies of other foods ranges only from 15 per cent to 23 per cent. It is interesting to note that the expense of retailing perishables in English towns and cities was found to be considerably less than that shown by the studies of American retailers. The generally higher margin on perishable articles, in comparison with the more staple foods, accords with what would be expected in consequence of the losses in physical volume incurred in retailing fruits and vegetables.

In the Harvard analysis of statements of 471 retail grocery stores in the United States and Canada for 1923, the principal items in store operation expense were found to be salaries and wages, rent, delivery, interest and losses from bad accounts, and miscellaneous expense for advertising, wrapping and sundry items. Salaries and wages were 10.5 per cent of the entire expense. The average expense for rent was 1.3 per cent of the net sales; for stores in large cities of 400,000 population or over, the rent item was slightly greater, being 1.7 per cent of net sales. The allowance for interest and losses from bad accounts together comprised 1.4 per cent, while delivery expense was 1.3 per cent. Advertising, wrapping and miscellaneous outlays absorbed 2.5 per cent. The total expense for the 471 stores was 17.3 per cent of net sales, and the net profit averaged 1.8 per cent, making the total margin to cover all expenses and profits 19.1 per cent. The overshadowing item of expense was that for salaries and wages. Rent and delivery expense, with interest charges and losses from bad accounts, were of minor importance in comparison with that of personnel. Salaries and wages, rent, and delivery expense, together accounted for about three-fourths of the total operating margin.

Relation of Size of Business to Operating Expense

In size of annual business transacted, there was a variation in the 471 stores of the Harvard Study from less than $30,000 to over $150,000. The stores were divided into five groups according to size of business. The stores having the lowest proportionate operating expense were those whose annual volume of business was between $50,000 and $100,000. The highest proportionate operating expense was in the smallest stores, those doing less than $30,000 of annual business. This group of small stores paid out 13 per cent of their gross receipts for wages, salaries and rent, whereas the larger-store group paid only 11.5 per cent for these items With the latter group there was an average net profit of 2.3 per cent, while the small-store group showed a slight net loss of 0.3 per cent.

An analysis of the retail meat trade in New York City[1] showed similarly a decline in gross margin with increased size of business. While stores doing $25,000 or less annual

[1] Data collected for 1917 by Federal Food Board; reported in *U. S. Dept. Agr. Bulletin 1317*, June, 1925, page 65.

business operated with an average gross margin of 18.4 per cent of sales, those with $50,000 to $100,000 had a gross margin of only 16 per cent. In the latter study, as in the Harvard Study, the rate of stock-turn, computed as the quotient of the year's total cost of goods and the inventory at the beginning of the year, increased regularly with the increase in total volume of sales. In the smallest stores of the Harvard Study the average stock-turn was only 8.2 times a year, while in the $50,000-$100,000 group it was 10.6 times, and in the $150,000 group it was 11.0 times. The larger the annual volume of business the more rapid was the movement of goods, and hence the smaller was the proportion of goods carried on hand. Moreover, the stores with the highest stock-turn were the ones with the lowest total expense, and the highest net profit.

From these studies it appears that small retail units moved their goods more slowly than the larger stores, and that they generally required a larger proportion of income for operation of the business. An undue proportion of the receipts of the small business units was absorbed by salaries, wages and rent. As the general movement of fruits and vegetables is necessarily much more rapid than that of staple groceries, the rate of stock-turn on perishable articles would seem to be even more closely associated with retailing expense. If this expense for perishables varies with the size of annual business as it does for groceries, then the small store seems to be at a particular disadvantage in distributing fruits and vegetables.

TABLE 7

DISTRIBUTION EXPENSE SHOWN IN SOME OTHER STUDIES

Agency making Study	Scope of Study	Commodity	Approximate Percentage of retailers' receipts
Harvard Bureau of Business Research [1]	471 grocery stores in U. S. and Canada (1923)	General Groceries	19
University of Wisconsin [2]	37 grocery stores of Madison (1919)	General Groceries [3]	15
University of Nebraska [4]	21 grocery stores in Lincoln and Omaha (1923)	General Groceries	23
Joint Commission of Agricultural Inquiry 67th Congress of U. S.[5]	Retailers throughout the U. S. (1921)	Groceries	19
		Meats (1918)	19
		Bread	18
		Milk	17
		Fresh eggs	14
		Oranges	24
		Potatoes	25
U. S. Department of Agriculture [6]	Retailers in 7 large American cities (1922–23), N. Y., Boston, Chicago, Minneapolis, Kansas City, New Orleans, San Francisco	Bread [7]	15
U. S. Department of Agriculture [8]	Washington, D. C. — unit grocery stores (1923)	Milk	18

[1] *Harvard Bulletin 41*—"Operating Expenses in Retail Grocery Stores in 1923."

[2] *Bulletin 324*—Wisconsin Agricultural Experiment Station, "What the Retailer Does with the Consumer's Dollar," by Macklin and McNall (Jan., 1921).

[3] Range in different stores 14 to 18 per cent.

[4] *Nebraska Studies in Business*, no. 10, "Operating Expense of Retail Grocery stores in Nebraska in 1923" (June, 1924).

[5] *House Report 408*, "Marketing and Distributions," pt. iv (1922).

[6] *U. S. Department of Agriculture Preliminary Report*, "An Analysis of the retail price of bread in seven cities, Oct. 1922 to Mar. 1923" (Feb., 1924).

[7] New York City; range in 7 cities is 11 to 17 per cent.

[8] *U. S. Department of Agriculture Preliminary Report*, "An Analysis of the Retail Price of a Quart of Milk Sold in Washington" (Feb., 1924).

TABLE 7—(*Continued*)

Agency making Study	Scope of Study	Commodity	Approximate Percentage of retailers' receipts
U. S. Department of Agriculture[1]	143 successful meat stores in Chicago, Cleveland and New York (1923)	Meat	19
U. S. Department of Agriculture[2]	3504 meat stores in 33 urban communities of the U. S. (1920)	Meat	19
U. S. Department of Agriculture[3]	64 meat stores in 5 Wisconsin Cities (1921)	Meat	22
U. S. Department of Agriculture[4]	282 retail stores in 26 states (1920)	Cranberries	22
U. S. Department of Agriculture[5]	Retailers of products of California Fruit Growers' Exchange (5 yrs., 1917–21)	Oranges	26
Massachusetts Department of Agriculture[6]	Various types of Boston retail stores (1920–21)	Maine Potatoes	21
U. S. Department of Agriculture[7]	Retailers in Boston, Chicago and Pittsburgh (1922–23)	Potatoes	37

[1] *U. S. Department of Agriculture Preliminary Report*, "Margins and Expenses in the Retail Meat Trade, Chicago, Cleveland and New York (May, 1924).

[2] *U. S. Department of Agriculture Bulletin 1317*, "Retail Marketing of Meats," June, 1925.

[3] *U. S. Department of Agriculture Preliminary Report*, "A Study of the Retail Meat Trade in Five Wisconsin Cities" (June, 1923).

[4] *U. S. Department of Agriculture Bulletin 1109*, "Sales Methods and Policies of a Growers' National Marketing Agency," A. Hobson and T. B. Chaney (Jan. 16, 1923).

[5] *U. S. Department of Agriculture Bulletin 1261*, "Operating Methods and Expense of Cooperative Citrus Fruit Marketing Agencies" (July 22, 1924).

[6] Unpublished manuscript, "The Marketing of Maine Potatoes in Massachusetts," E. C. Shoup (June, 1922).

[7] *U. S. Department of Agriculture Preliminary Report*, "An Analysis of the Retail Price of Potatoes Grown in Maine, Minnesota, Wisconsin and Michigan, and Sold in Boston, Chicago and Pittsburgh, Season 1923" (March, 1924).

TABLE 7—(*Concluded*)

Agency making Study	Scope of Study	Commodity	Approximate Percentage of retailers' receipts
New England Research Council [1]	Various types of retail stores (1922–23)	Onions	36
New York State Food Commission & Federal Food Board [2]	128 representative grocery stores in Greater New York (1917)	Groceries	16
New York State Food Commission & Federal Food Board	58 representative grocery stores in Greater New York (1917)	Potatoes Onions	23 40
U. S. Department of Agriculture [3]	Selected retail stores in Boston (Oct., 1921–Mar., 1922)	Cabbage	42
Massachusetts Department of Agriculture [4]	Various types of retail stores in metropolitan Boston (1921)	9 selected vegetables [5]	36
Massachusetts Department of Agriculture [6]	Various types of retail stores in metropolitan Boston (1922–23)	9 selected vegetables [7]	36
U. S. Department of Agriculture [8]	5 representative stalls in Centre Market, Washington, D. C., (5 weeks of 1923)	15 seasonable fruits and vegetables	40
British Ministry of Agriculture [9]	65 private retailers and co-operative societies in English towns and cities (1923)	Fresh fruits and vegetables	20

[1] Unpublished manuscript, "Marketing Connecticut Valley onions."

[2] N. Y. State Department of Farms Markets—*Circular 240*—"Retail Grocery Stores," 1923.

[3] *U. S. Department of Agriculture Bulletin 1242*, "Marketing Cabbage," Sept. 2, 1924.

[4] Unpublished manuscript, "A Study of the Percentage Margins at which selected farm products are handled by various types of retail stores in Metropolitan Boston" by B. B. Smith, June, 1922.

[5] Simple mean for 9 articles; range is 21 to 59 per cent.

[6] Unpublished manuscript, "A Study of the Percentage Margins at which selected farm products are handled by various types of retail stores in Metropolitan Boston" by Allen M. James, May, 1923.

[7] Simple mean—range 28 to 61 per cent.

[8] *U. S. Department of Agriculture*, unpublished report by A. V. Swarthout, Bureau of Agricultural Economics, "Retailers' Margins on Fruits and Vegetables in Center Market, Washington" (1923).

[9] British Ministry of Agriculture and Fisheries, Committee on Distribution and Prices of Agricultural Produce, "Interim Report on Fruits and Vegetables," 1923.

CHAPTER III

Scope and Method of Analysis

The particular object of the present study is to locate the more significant factors that account for variations in the expense of distributing perishable fruits and vegetables within the metropolitan area. This object is attempted by means of comparisons of this expense under different stated conditions of city distribution. The immediate problem is therefore to determine the extent of the spreads in prices under the various conditions that are to be considered.

In attempting to measure price spreads, the first step was to collect an adequate amount of original price data that would be representative of prevailing metropolitan conditions. These data were then refined and classified, and the results were tabulated in preparation for the analyses presented in Chapter IV and Chapter V of this study.

NATURE AND EXTENT OF DATA

The data collected originally for this purpose comprised nearly fifteen thousand sets of original price observations, extending over a continuous period of sixteen months, commencing the first week in February, 1923, and extending through May, 1924. These data were gathered weekly in several sections of the metropolitan area. The variety of articles reported was wide enough to include both staples and specialties of the various fruits and vegetables entering into city consumption. Upwards of fifty stores assisted in supplying the retail price data, although most of the quotations were secured from thirty of these. Grocery stores and fruit-vegetable stores in Manhattan, Brooklyn, Bronx, Newark, Passaic, and Elizabeth were included in order to represent diverse sections of the metropolitan area. The approximate location of these stores, and their relation to sources of supply, are shown by the small dark circles and connecting lines in Figure 2 (page 32). Prices prevailing in the wholesale and jobbing markets were collected weekly throughout the data period for dates corresponding to the retail quotations.

METHOD OF COLLECTION

Retail quotations were collected by regularly accredited reporters, principally housewives and representatives of women's organizations in the localities surveyed.[1] These reporters volunteered their services as a matter of public spirit and of personal interest in the project. During the latter part of the study they were paid a small weekly compensation for the time required in collecting the quotations. The stores were mainly shops in each reporter's neighborhood where the family trading was done. Selling prices were collected on Friday morning of each week in each case and were recorded with the store designation on a printed report form, which was then mailed under Government frank to the headquarters of the study in New York City. Each reporter interviewed the store proprietor or a clerk, and there entered on the report form a careful description of the variety, grade, and size offered for sale, with the price of each commodity reported.

Jobbing prices were collected by members of the research staff of the United States Bureau of Agricultural Economics, in the four jobbing markets, Harlem, Gansevoort, Wallabout and Newark. Three to five representative jobbers in each

[1] See list of assisting organizations in preface.

of these markets were interviewed each Friday morning of the period between the hours of eight and eleven o'clock, after the bulk of their day's business was over. Prices quoted by each jobber for specified standard varieties and grades were recorded for each week in a written report. The mean commodity prices in each jobbing market were matched against the corresponding retail prices of stores supplied from the given jobbing source.

Wholesale prices were obtained from the daily New York market report of the United States Department of Agriculture for Thursday of each week, one day's interval being allowed for distribution of goods from wholesale market to jobbing market and to retail stores. These quotations were obtained for prevailing standard grades and varieties of fruits and vegetables, from representative wholesalers. The wholesale prices for California oranges were taken from the auction sale records published by a New York auction company.

SELECTION OF REPRESENTATIVE STORES

The selection of stores was made to include varying types of management, of clientele, and of selling policy in each locality. A description of each store was placed on file, indicating whether it was a chain store or an independent unit, whether it carried fruits and vegetables in addition to a general line of groceries or specialized only in perishable goods, whether the store granted credit and made deliveries, or operated on a cash and carry basis, classification of its trade as high-class, middle-class, or low-price, and the jobbing market from which the retailer secured his supplies. The descriptions supplied by the reporters were verified on the part of the writer by personal visits to the stores and interviews with their proprietors.

CHOICE AND SUBDIVISIONS OF COMMODITIES

The selection of commodities included the articles of major consumption and those having various marketing characteristics and typical dietary uses. The choice was restricted to such goods as are prevailingly sold by retail stores, and which are sufficiently standardized to admit of ready identification and comparison. With these points in mind, four kinds of fruits and five of vegetables were chosen:

Fruits	*Vegetables*
Apples	White Potatoes
Oranges	Sweet Potatoes
Peaches	Onions
Cantaloupes	Lettuce
	Cabbage

These nine commodities come to the New York market from a wide variety of sources at various seasons of the year. Some of them vary considerably in type of shipping package, in variety, and in the manner in which they are sold at retail. New potatoes, for example, come to market early in the season from the southern states and from Bermuda, packed in barrels, while the later crop from the northern states is marketed in sacks or in bulk. Consumers buy the early high-priced potatoes in smaller quantities than the lower-priced main crop. There are variety differences in onions, the principal consumption as a regular article of diet being of yellow onions while white onions are sold for more sparing special uses. Lettuce comes to market from different producing regions in two distinct varieties, each of which appeals to certain types of trade. There is a similar variation in cabbage. The early southern cabbage has smaller heads than the later northern; hence the average weight per retail sale is less, since cabbage is prevailingly sold by the single head. Apples appear in the market both in barrels and in boxes. The former are used chiefly for cooking and are retailed chiefly by weight or measure, while boxed apples are usually sold by count for eating out of hand.

Because of distinctions which affect the manner in which these commodities are distributed to consumers, five of the selected articles were further subdivided. With these subdivisions the study contains the following fourteen classes: Northern potatoes, southern potatoes, boxed apples, barreled apples, eastern lettuce, western lettuce, northern cabbage, southern cabbage, yellow onions, white onions, sweet potatoes, oranges, peaches, cantaloupes.

MARKETING CHARACTERISTICS

Northern potatoes include all those usually designated as main crop. These are produced in the states north of Virginia, coming chiefly from Long Island and other portions of New York State, from Maine, Michigan, Pennsylvania, Wisconsin, and other scattered sources. They are received in New York in carlots and auto-truck loads either in bulk or in sacks of 150, 165 and 180 pounds. They are sold in the wholesale and jobbing markets by the sack, the price quotations varying with the number of pounds per sack, and with variety and source.

Southern potatoes comprise those produced in Virginia and areas south of it, and also the receipts from Delaware and Maryland during June and July. They start coming into the New York Market from Bermuda in January or February. These are followed successively by the crops from Florida, the Carolinas, and Virginia. A small quantity of second crop potatoes marketed from Virginia during the early winter months is included. Southern potatoes are marketed mainly in double-headed barrels, but a small portion comes in crates at the beginning of the season.

The basic unit adopted for both northern and southern potatoes is the hundred-weight, on account of the variability of different package units, and to meet the necessity of bringing all to a common weight basis for price comparisons.

Apples are classified as boxed or barreled, according to the kind of package in which they are shipped to market. This varies according to source. *Boxed apples* come chiefly from the Pacific Coast states of Washington, Oregon and California and from Montana. The main varieties are Jonathan, Spitzenberg, Delicious, Winesap and Newton Pippin. The fruit is packed uniformly in 40 pound boxes, graded according to size and ranging in contents from 64 to 163 fruits per box. They are classified according to quality as Extra Fancy, Fancy and C-Grade. Although retailed principally by count, boxed apples are sold frequently by weight or measure.

Barreled apples come to the metropolitan market chiefly from New York State, New England, Pennsylvania, Virginia and West Virginia. The principal varieties are Baldwin, Greening, McIntosh, York Imperial, Newton and Albermarle Pippin; but numerous other kinds are marketed during the fall months. Although most of the winter varieties from the eastern states are shipped in barrels, quite a proportion of fall varieties is marketed in bushel baskets. All this eastern fruit is included in the classification as barreled apples. They are graded for market according to diameter of fruit, into 2½ inch, 2¾, and 3 inch, and are packed mainly in two qualities as "A" or Fancy, and "B" or Choice. The eastern fruit is retailed chiefly by weight or measure and is used mainly for cooking. Most of the quotations included in the study were for Baldwins and Greenings.

The classification of *lettuce* as *Eastern* and *Western* is based primarily upon a difference in variety, but this coincides also with the regions where it is produced. The lettuce coming into the New York market from the eastern and southern states is prevailingly of the variety known in the trade as "Big Boston." This starts coming from Florida in December. As the season advances, its producing area moves northward progressively through South and North Carolina, Virginia, Delaware and Maryland, to New Jersey and New York State. The southern crop is marketed chiefly in hampers of 1½ bushel or 1¼ bushel, containing from 30 to 45 heads. The New Jersey and New York State crop is packed in uniform crates containing two dozen heads each. A slight portion of hot-house grown eastern lettuce is also marketed in 2-dozen crates. In this study prices for eastern lettuce were all converted to a uniform basis, that of the 1½ bushel hamper containing an average of 36 medium-sized heads.

The lettuce produced in the western states is of the variety known in the trade as "Simpson" or "Iceberg". It comes chiefly from California, Arizona, Idaho and Texas, and is packed in crates containing from 3½ to 5 dozen heads, the number varying according to size and to producing section. In this analysis the standard western crate is regarded as containing 4 dozen medium-sized heads. The western lettuce is slightly larger per head than the eastern Boston variety.

The classification of *cabbage* into northern and southern covers a variety distinction as well as a distinction in source and manner of shipment. *Northern cabbage* includes the main crop produced in the northern states, chiefly in New York, also that imported from Europe during the early spring months. Its marketing period extends from August or September to March or April. It comes to the New York market chiefly in carlots, and is sold by wholesalers and jobbers in bulk, or in sacks or barrels containing from 100 pounds to 130 pounds.

Southern Cabbage is produced in states south of New

Jersey, and comes to the New York market chiefly from Florida, the Carolinas, Virginia and Texas. It is shipped in hampers and in crates holding from 80 to 120 pounds. That received in the market from January to April, is mainly with pointed heads of the Wakefield variety. Shipments during May and June are chiefly of the flat type. The size of heads of cabbage varies considerably, ranging from 1½ or 2 pounds for the early small Wakefield to 4 or 5 pounds for the large solid northern or imported Danish. Prices for both northern and southern cabbage have been converted in this study to a hundred-weight basis.

The subdivision of *onions* into two groups,—*yellow* and *white*—is based upon differences in type and in the manner in which they are used by consumers. The principal supply is the *yellow* type, and it includes two varieties. The main crop consists of the globe variety produced in New York State, New Jersey, Ohio, Indiana and Massachusetts. This is shipped uniformly in 100 pound sacks, excepting the small portion produced in New Jersey, which is marketed in hampers containing about 50 pounds each. This supply is in the New York market from August to April. The yellow globe variety includes also the onions imported from Egypt during the late spring, and some from Holland. The other variety of yellow onions, known in the trade as the Texas-Bermuda type, is flatter than the globe onion, and comes chiefly from Texas and northern Mexico. It is sold in the New York market in standard crates containing from 45 to 50 pounds each. The Texas crop is marketed during April, May and June. A small portion comes also from Bermuda in the early spring. The analysis has not taken into consideration the large Spanish onions.

White Onions are classified separtely from yellow onions because of the contrast in their consumption uses. They are more of a specialty in household use. They are preferred by certain elements of the population, particularly by the Jews, for pickling and for boiling. This vegetable is classified in three sizes, known in the trade as large, boilers, and picklers. Picklers and boilers often command a considerable premium over the price for the large size. White onions are produced mainly in the northern states which grow the yellow onions. They are marketed in 100 pound sacks and are sold in the wholesale and jobbing markets similarly to the northern yellow onions. A small portion of Texas-Bermuda onions, of the crystal wax variety, is also included as white onions. In the absence of official records of volume, the consumption of white onions was estimated as ten per cent of the total onion receipts.

Sweet Potatoes appear in the New York market most of the months of the year. The chief sources are New Jersey and Virginia, with some shipments from Delaware and Maryland. The Virginia crop comes to the market in barrels, but that from New Jersey is marketed in bushel hampers. The Virginia crop is not of much importance excepting in the fall months; hence the price data are mostly for the New Jersey crop. For convenience and uniformity the volumes were converted to a uniform hundred-weight basis.

The supply of *oranges* comes to New York from California, Florida and Porto Rico. Florida oranges were included at the beginning of the analysis, but were discontinued on account of difficulties in identifying brands and in determining representative wholesale prices for the large number of diverse brands appearing in the market. The data, therefore, are for California oranges only. These are marketed under local brand names as well as general trade names. Like boxed apples, they are packed uniformly in boxes and are graded in several standard sizes. The data are mainly for Sunkist oranges, and are for the sizes most widely sold in retail stores.

The supply of *peaches* in the New York market comes from a number of sources, and is of several varieties. The principal sources are Georgia, New Jersey, New York and Michigan. The Georgia crop is marketed in crates or 6-basket carriers, each basket containing 4 quarts. Part of the Jersey crop is marketed in the same way, and part in bushel baskets. The New York and Michigan crops are shipped mostly in half-bushel hampers. The Georgia crop begins to appear in the market in May or June, and continues until late July or August, when the New Jersey crop comes in. This is followed in September and October by the main crops from New York State and Michigan. In computing the prices for fruit from these various sources, with their varying containers, all were converted to a 24-quart-carrier basis.

Although *cantaloupes* come from numerous sources, the largest quantities are received from California, Arizona, New Mexico and Colorado. A considerable portion comes also from the eastern states,—from the Carolinas, Tennessee, Delaware and New Jersey. This commodity is marketed in crates of several sizes, the most common size containing from 36 to 45 melons. There is also a "pony" crate of smaller dimensions, which contains a similar number of smaller melons. The standard "flat" crate contains one tier of from 9 to 15 cantaloupes. The eastern melon crate is the same size as the western, but the eastern melons generally do not run as large. All of the data were converted to the basis of the standard crate with its mean contents estimated at 40 medium-sized melons.

REPRESENTATIVENESS OF PRICE QUOTATIONS

All possible care was taken to obtain price quotations that were truly representative of the different marketing stages. The reporters of retail prices were carefully trained and instructed in identifying varieties, sizes and qualities of articles reported, so that their reports would be uniform. Actual purchases by customers, or prices posted in the stores, were the basis of the retail quotations. These were stated in terms of the small retail quantities prevailingly sold, i. e. per pound, quart, peck, basket, head, dozen, individual fruit or the usual multiples, or for an advertised lump quantity such as 25 cents' worth. Each retail quotation was converted to an equivalent retail price per shipping package or hundred-weight, by multiplying the quoted price by the computed number of sales of the reported quantity in the gross commodity package. Wholesale and jobbing prices were reported directly in the same gross units,—by the crate, box, hamper, barrel, sack or hundred-weight; hence they required no conversions.

Against each retail price was matched the proper wholesale and jobbing figure, so that the stages of city distribution formed for each quotation a triple price series. In the case of chain stores, jobbing prices were omitted because of the prevailing practice in these stores of direct purchase at wholesale. Very careful judgment was applied in order that each part of a price series should represent an identical kind and quality of commodity. By basing the original quotations on standard varieties and grades prevalent in the city markets, the possible error due to commodity variations in condition, source and type of container, was reduced to a minimum.

POSSIBLE SOURCES OF ERROR

Three possible sources of error exist in regarding these quotations as typical of actual marketing practice in the metropolitan area, namely

Failure of individual quotations to represent actual sales.

Failure of the selected average quotations to be truly representative of individual quotations.

Failure of the data as a whole to be typical of general marketing conditions.

Derivation of a single wholesale price or jobbing price that will be typical of uniform or identical goods on a given date is difficult because of the sudden price changes that take place in the wholesale and jobbing markets, even within the space of a few hours. Variations in the prices charged by different dealers in the same market increase this difficulty. Retail prices are subject to less variation than the others, because they change more slowly.

The fact that the retail quotations represent actual sales minimizes the inaccuracy of using them for statistical analysis. The wholesale quotations, being from official reports of sales by principal dealers in the wholesale market, are as accurately representative as any that were available. The greatest possibility of error arises in the jobbers' quotations, because of the number and diversity of jobbers and the sensitiveness of the jobbers' market to sudden changes in the wholesale market. These jobbing prices, however, do not affect the major part of the study, since this deals mainly with differences between wholesale and retail prices only. Jobbers' quotations are employed only in the analysis of different forms of store operation to calculate the retailer's portion.

In the absence of bias in obtaining the retail, jobbing and wholesale quotations, the possible errors arising from inaccuracy on any particular day or week [1] would tend to compensate one another in the succession of individual quotations for different dates covered in the study. Errors on the positive side would tend to be offset by errors on the negative side, so that the price averages which are used should be a fairly accurate representation of prices actually prevailing. The methods pursued, the care taken in selecting samples of

[1] See *Tests of Validity of Quotations in Appendix*, pp. 164-5.

prices, the variety of localities and store types and general conditions, the length of time covered, and the volume of data secured, unite to make the results of this study as truly representative of distribution conditions in the New York metropolitan area, as would be possible in any study of similar scope.

TABULATION OF RESULTS.

Each retail quotation for a given date was transcribed from the card on which it was reported, with the store designation and descriptive details, to a large common data sheet where it was entered in the proper commodity section, with the converted retail price. In other parallel columns were then entered the corresponding jobbing and wholesale quotations. The following specimen entry shows the details that were included in each completed set of prices.

BOXED APPLES—MAY 9, 1924

Code No. of store	Jobbing market source	Description	Reported retail quotation	Converted retail price per box	Jobbing price	Wholesale price
155	Harlem	Winesap Extra Fancy Size 113	6 for 25 c.	$4.70	$2.50	$2.15

To facilitate the work of classifying and tabulating the data, the details of each set of price quotations, with its computed percentage margin,[1] were entered from the data sheets in code on a punched tabulating card. Each card thus contained complete information for one set of prices. The cards were then sorted into the desired classes and their results were tabulated by groups with the Hollerith machine. A small portion of the original number of 14,806 cards had

[1] See footnote *infra*, p. 71.

to be discarded because of incompleteness, so that the number used in the commodity analyses was slightly less than fourteen thousand quotations. The number and distribution of these sets of price quotations by commodities are shown in Table 8.

TABLE 8

NUMBER OF PRICE QUOTATIONS USED IN COMMODITY ANALYSES, NEW YORK METROPOLITAN AREA, FEBRUARY, 1923–MAY, 1924

Commodity	*Total quotations* [1]
California oranges	2,017
Yellow onions	1,757
Northern potatoes	1,606
Boxed apples	1,435
Barreled apples	1,284
Eastern lettuce	1,276
Sweet potatoes	1,252
Northern cabbage	774
Southern cabbage	688
Southern potatoes	538
Western lettuce	484
Cantaloupes	353
Peaches	270
White onions	237
Total—14 commodities	13,971

CHOICE OF AVERAGES

Selections of the most truly typical average for analyzing the different groups of data was made after considering the respective merits of the median of the percentage margins,[1] the mean of the percentage margins, and the percentage margin computed from the mean wholesale and mean retail prices.

The *median* margin, which is the middle item of an arrayed

[1] Totals here are slightly smaller than in appendix, p. 153, some cards having been omitted, as for example, in cases where jobbers' quotations were not obtainable.

group, was favored because this minimizes the influence of extremely small or extremely large items. This is especially important when the group of data is small. With highly varying items, however, the median is a poor indicator of their general tendency; and it is indefinite in cases where the middle term in an array falls between two widely differing items.

The *mean* margin, which is a simple arithmetic average computed by dividing the sum of individual margins of a group by the number of items, is a satisfactory average where the data are numerous. In a small group, the disproportionate influence of extreme items makes it unreliable. Moreover, difficulties arise in determining the mean for a group where occasional negative items occur.

The third form of margin to be considered was that computed from the *means of the respective prices*. This is a quotient obtained by dividing the difference between mean retail price and mean wholesale price by the mean retail price.[1]

Each of these three forms of averages was thoroughly tested, to ascertain which one was most generally representative of the various groups of data. The percentage margin, computed from the mean wholesale and mean retail prices, proved to be the most representative as well as the most generally consistent of the three. Throughout the subsequent analyses, therefore, the means of the prices themselves are employed as the basis of comparison. Wherever the percentage margin is used, it is computed from these respective mean prices.[2]

1 See footnote *infra*, p. 71.

2 See footnote *infra*, p. 71.

ADJUSTMENT OF PRICES FOR SHRINKAGE

Shrinkage in physical contents of packages while in process of distribution makes it necessary to allow for this factor in computing the retail prices and the margins resultant from them. Some correction was necessary, also, for discrepancies in converting the original quotations to a package basis. Adjustments for shrinkage, and corrections in the retail prices, were made by multiplying the mean

TABLE 9

ADJUSTMENTS FOR SHRINKAGE IN RETAILING, NEW YORK METROPOLITAN AREA

Commodity	Shipping unit	Gross weight per unit	Amount usually retailed	Percentage of shipping unit retailed
		Pounds	Pounds	Per cent
Northern potatoes	cwt.	100	95	95
Southern potatoes	cwt.	100	92	92
California oranges	box	75	75	100
Peaches	crate	35	33	94
Sweet potatoes	cwt.	100	90	90
Cantaloupes	crate	60	60	100
Boxed apples	box	40	40	100
Southern cabbage	cwt.	100	90	90
Barreled apples	bbl.	150	135	90
Eastern lettuce	hamper	34	34	100
Western lettuce	crate	48	48	100
Yellow onions	cwt.	100	95	95
Northern cabbage	cwt.	100	90	90
White onions	cwt.	100	95	95

retail package price of each commodity by the percentage of the wholesale volume actually sold at retail. This percentage is shown in the last column of Table 9. The proportions were verified by figures and statements from representative retailers in various parts of the metropolitan area. This item includes only physical shrinkage in handling, and corrections for the original retail calculations. It does not include any allowance for waste or deterioration. No adjustment was required in the wholesale or jobbing quotations, for these were based upon gross-package quantities irrespective of weight, or upon actual weight when goods were sold by the hundredweight.

REPRESENTATIVE PRICES AND MARGINS

The composite means of retail and wholesale prices of each commodity for the entire period embraced in this study, are shown in Table 10. These generalized averages were used to determine the representative or typical margin of each commodity as a whole. The retail prices are weighted according to importance of the different store types,[1] and are also adjusted for shrinkage in retailing. The average distribution expense per package is the difference between mean retail price and mean wholesale price. It is expressed as a percentage of the retail price in the last column. These average prices and percentage margins are the basic figures used in the commodity analyses in Chapter IV.

TABLE 10

MEAN PRICES AND MARGINS, NEW YORK METROPOLITAN AREA, FEBRUARY, 1923–MAY, 1924

Commodity	Physical Unit	Mean retail price	Mean wholesale price	Percentage margin
Northern potatoes	cwt.	$3.87	$2.43	37 per cent
Southern potatoes	cwt.	6.76	4.18	38 " "
California oranges	box	8.21	4.86	41 " "
Peaches	24 qt. crt.	3.97	2.20	45 " "
Sweet potatoes	cwt.	8.00	4.44	45 " "
Cantaloupes	std. crt.	4.57	2.45	46 " "
Boxed apples	box	4.35	2.33	46 " "
Southern cabbage	cwt.	8.42	4.42	48 " "
Barreled apples	bbl.	10.76	5.53	49 " "
Eastern lettuce	1½ bu. hpr.	4.43	2.16	51 " "
Western lettuce	4 dz. crt.	7.05	3.37	52 " "
Yellow onions	cwt.	6.70	3.17	53 " "
Northern cabbage	cwt.	4.68	1.96	58 " "
White onions	cwt.	8.59	3.22	63 " "

[1] See *supra*, p. 25 and Appendix Tables, p. 137.

INTERPRETATION OF PRICE-SPREADS AND MARGINS

The expense of distribution may be expressed as a price-spread, as a " margin ", or as a " mark-up ". The spread between the wholesale value and the retail value of a stated quantity of goods is ordinarily indicated in dollars and cents. The consumer regards the value of the goods he buys as based upon the retail price he pays the storekeeper. To him the price-spread is logically associated with the retail price. This spread, in the consumer's mind, is included in the price which he pays for the retailer's services. By the merchant, however, the price-spread is considered as a mark-up on the cost of his goods. It is an addition to the price he pays at wholesale, and is external to it.

When the " margin " or the " mark-up " is expressed in dollars and cents, in relation to given retail or wholesale prices for a stated quantity of goods, naturally the two are identical. Each indicates the monetary amount required for distribution of the commodity,—the former from the consumer's point of view, the latter from that of the merchant.

A flat comparison of money spreads for different articles is meaningless, because of differences in their quantity units. Comparison of a spread of 50 cents on a box of apples, with a spread of $1.00 on a barrel of southern potatoes, has no statistical significance. If all commodity prices were reduced to a common quantity basis, such as a hundred-weight, comparison of monetary spreads would still have little meaning, because of differences in the specific value of different articles. A spread of 50 cents on a commodity worth $5.00 a hundred-weight is quite different from a similar spread on an article worth $3.00 per hundred pounds.

In order to make the price-spreads comparable for a series of commodities, they are therefore expressed as price percentages. When price-spread is expressed as a percentage of retail or of wholesale price, there is a radical difference between margin and mark-up, because of the different bases used in computing the percentages.[1] The higher the percentage margin, the wider is its divergence from the percentage mark-up, as shown in Table 11.

ADDITIONAL WORKING DATA

In addition to the collected price data, the following information was used in connection with the subsequent analyses: (a) total 1923 carlot receipts of each commodity,[2] (b) physical contents per package,[3] and per car,[4] (c) the

[1] The *percentage margin* is expressed mathematically by $\frac{R-W}{R}$, where R is the retail price and W is the wholesale price. The spread is the difference between R and W. The spread divided by the retail price gives the margin as a percentage of this retail price. Similarly the *percentage mark-up is* $\frac{R-W}{W}$, i. e., the spread divided by the wholesale price. Hence the percentage margin is always smaller than the percentage mark-up, because R is greater than W, unless it is assumed that the retailer sells at a loss.

In the analyses that follow, the percentage margin for each group of data is calculated from the difference between the mean retail and mean wholesale price of that group. It is derived from the mathematical formula $\frac{\Sigma R-\Sigma W}{\Sigma R}$ where ΣR is the *sum* of the retail prices, and ΣW is the *sum* of the wholesale prices for the same group of data. This formula is equivalent to that employing the *mean* retail and *mean* wholesale prices, $\frac{\frac{\Sigma R}{N}-\frac{\Sigma W}{N}}{\frac{\Sigma R}{N}}$ in which N is the number of observations in the group. When numerator and denominator of the latter expression are both multiplied by N, it becomes identical with the preceding formula.

[2] From *U. S. D. A. Market News Circular*, February 15, 1924.

[3] From *U. S. D. A. Farmers Bulletin 1196*, "Standard Containers for Fruits and Vegetables."

[4] From *U. S. D. A. Bureau of Agricultural Economics Revised Form FV33*, "Table of packages per carload."

TABLE 11

RELATION BETWEEN PERCENTAGE MARGIN AND PERCENTAGE MARK-UP

Commodity	City margin Percentage of retail price	City mark-up Percentage of wholesale price
	Per cent	Per cent
Northern potatoes	37	59
Southern potatoes	38	62
California oranges	41	69
Sweet potatoes	45	80
Peaches	45	81
Cantaloupes	46	87
Boxed apples	46	87
Southern cabbage	48	91
Barreled apples	49	95
Eastern lettuce	51	105
Western lettuce	52	109
Yellow onions	53	111
Northern cabbage	58	139
White onions	63	167
Weighted mean	44.6	80.5

average size of the retail sale.[1] With the aid of these facts, the following statistical information was derived by simple mathematical calculation [2] for each commodity:

Total 1923 wholesale value
Total 1923 retail value
Total 1923 distribution expense
Mean wholesale price per car
Mean retail price per car
Mean distribution expense per car
Mean wholesale price per pound
Mean retail price per pound
Value of mean retail sale
Price-spread per mean retail sale.

[1] Based upon information from representative retailers, see p. 77.

[2] These various quantities, with their methods of calculation, are presented in the Appendix tables (pp. 137-147).

The total wholesale and retail values of each commodity are derived from the original price quotations. The assumption was made that the reported volume of each commodity was distributed entirely through the types of retailers that are specially studied in this report. This ignores the other agencies of distribution—pushcarts, hotels, etc.,—whose functions are not here considered. This does not affect the analysis, however, nor the soundness of the conclusions. Total wholesale value is the product of the mean wholesale price per package or hundred-weight, the number of packages or the weight per car, and the number of cars received in 1923. The total retail value is similarly the product of the mean retail price (adjusted for shrinkage in selling), the number of quoted retail units per package or hundred-weight, the number of packages or the weight per car, and the number of cars. Total distribution expense is the difference between total wholesale and total retail values. The price per car is the product of the price per package or hundred-weight and the number of these per car. The price per pound is a quotient of the price per package and the number of pounds per package. The value of the retail sale is a product of retail price per pound and the mean number of pounds per retail sale.

DISTRIBUTION FACTORS CONSIDERED

The original classifications of data embraced (1) the kind of commodity, (2) the type of store management, (3) the store policy in regard to credit and delivery service, (4) the clientele or type of trade, (5) the locality in respect to market sources, and (6) the status of the store in respect to specialization. In the preliminary general inspection of the average margins for the groups of data within these classifications, the divergence between the averages readily showed which factors of distribution were of principal significance. The widest divergence in average margins was among the groups of data for different kinds of commodities. The next widest was among the store classifications, based upon differences in management and in selling policy. The other factors were of lesser consequence.[1] The statistical analyses are therefore concentrated upon studies of the first three factors.

The analysis of commodity differences is presented in Chapter IV. The analysis of differences due to store management and to contrasts in credit and delivery policy is given in Chapter V. The theoretical implications arising from the analyses are considered in Chapter VI, and in Chapter VII are presented the conclusions growing out of the entire study. A full record of tabulations of data used in these analyses is presented in the statistical appendix.

[1] See *infra*, p. 94, in regard to the factor of specialization.

CHAPTER IV

Commodity Contrasts

In the series of fourteen commodities the factor having greatest significance, as shown by differences in distribution expense, was found to be the nature of the commodity marketed. The range in the margins extended from a minimum of 37 per cent of the retail price for northern potatoes to a maximum of 63 per cent for white onions. Such a wide divergence in the portion of consumers' outlays absorbed in distributing different articles of similar general characteristics, requires careful explanation. What variable marketing qualities of the fourteen commodities are adequate to explain these contrasts?

POSSIBLE FACTORS AFFECTING DISTRIBUTION EXPENSES

In searching for an answer to this question, the following factors were suggested as possibly capable of influencing the manner of handling the various articles sufficiently to establish the differences in margins:

The total amount of commodity annually marketed
The total annual value of the commodity
The specific value per unit of goods
Regularity of supply
Relative perishability
Variability in wholesale price

Numerous detailed tests of the data were made in turn to ascertain the extent of association between these commodity factors and the respective percentage margins. In applying the tests, many comparative tables were constructed, and numerous scatter diagrams and curves were plotted to discover relationships. Although a limited degree of association was found with some of the suggested factors, the relation was not sufficiently regular or uniform to afford an adequate explanation of the margin differences. It was necessary, therefore, to seek further for contrasts in the manner of distributing the various articles.

DIFFERENCES IN SERVICE REQUIREMENTS

It was suggested that variations might exist in the amount of service required in distributing a dollar's worth of different commodities, and that such variations might suffice to explain the margin differences. It is an obvious fact that the amount of goods taken at a time by an individual customer bears very little relation to the amount of time and service required from the retailer. A customer who purchases a very small quantity of goods requires practically as much of the store-keeper's or clerk's time as does the person who makes a large purchase. Hence it is a reasonable supposition that the selling expense per retail sale should be fairly uniform, irrespective of the size of the sale.

In seeking a criterion that would be a measure of possible variations in service requirements, attention was directed to the fact that the size of the average retail sale differs materially with different commodities. This variation in size of the retail sale was the key that provided the needed explanation. The prevailing size of the consumer's individual purchase is found to determine in large measure the proportion of the consumer's outlay which is absorbed in the distribution process.

SIZE OF RETAIL SALE AS A MEASURE OF SERVICE REQUIREMENTS

A special unit of measure is required to express correctly the amount of service given in selling merchandise of different kinds. This unit is not any of the prevailing standard units of weight or of volume,—such as the pound or quart or dozen,—in which selling prices are usually stated. This new measure of service is the *standard retail sale.* In terms of physical quantity, the size of this unit varies considerably with different articles in the commodity series. In terms of service rendered, as expressive of the expense of retailing, however, this unit is fairly constant. A combination of variations in value of the retail sale which attend the variations in its physical size, with a fairly uniform selling expense per sale, is found to yield the differences observed in the percentage margins of different commodities.

While retail prices are stated usually in terms of a uniform physical unit, such as the pound, quart, head, dozen or similar measure, the retailer makes his actual sales not in such individual units, but in various multiples of them. To be sure, a great deal of variation exists in the individual sales within a single commodity, because of differences in the buying habits of different customers. Yet the practice of the trade in general is sufficiently regular to establish a prevailing size of sale that may be regarded as typical for a given commodity.

Careful inquiries were made in the retail trade to ascertain the prevailing quantities of different commodities bought at a time by consumers. These inquiries embraced the broad experience of two metropolitan chain-store systems, of several independent retailers, and of a number of individual families whose purchases were recorded in the original price data. From such diverse and representative sources, the prevailing range in size of sale was ascertained quite definitely for each commodity. The mid-point in this range was then taken to indicate the typical or standard retail sale. Use of the mid-point is justified as an approximate indicator of the prevailing size of sale, in view of the fact that extremes, such as unusually small sales and unusually large sales were excluded from the ranges given. It is recognized that this method involves some degree of approximation, but in the absence of more definite data for arriving at specific accuracy, which could be obtained only by recording exact details of a large number of individual sales under representative conditions, the method here employed is justified as the best that was available.

The prevailing range and the mid-point for each of the fourteen commodities, expressed uniformly as pounds, are shown in the first two columns of Table 12. The mid-points vary in the series of fourteen articles from a minimum of 1½ pounds for western lettuce to a maximum of 6½ pounds for northern potatoes thus leaving a range of 5 pounds throughout the series. The mean size of sale for the whole series, weighted according to the importance of each commodity, is approximately 3¼ pounds. The difference between the smallest and largest size of sale is thus not far from twice the mean for the series.

Now in retail selling the significance of variations in size of sale lies in the relation this bears to the monetary value of the goods disposed of in a single transaction. The value of the retail sale is determined by two variables. One of these is the physical quantity disposed of; the other variable is the price per unit of goods. This is here computed on a pound basis to correspond with the uniform weight basis used to express the size of sale. The retail price per pound for each commodity, as shown in the third column of the table, was calculated from the mean of the original quotations, converted to a package or hundred-weight basis, and thence to the mean price per pound.[1] The value of the standard retail sale is the product of this mean retail price per pound and the number of pounds in the standard retail sale. It is shown for each commodity in the fourth column of Table 12. The price spread in terms of the retail sale is

TABLE 12

SIZE AND VALUE OF STANDARD RETAIL SALE, PERCENTAGE MARGINS AND PRICE SPREAD PER SALE FOR FOURTEEN COMMODITIES IN ALL STORE TYPES. NEW YORK METROPOLITAN AREA, FEBRUARY, 1923–MAY, 1924

Commodity	Prevailing range in size of retail sale	Mid-point of range	Mean retail price per pound[2]	Value of standard retail sale	Percentage margin	Price-spread per standard retail sale[3]
	Pounds	Pounds	Cents	Cents	Per cent	Cents
Northern potatoes.	5 to 8	6.50	4.1	26.7	37	9.9
Southern potatoes.	3 to 4.5	3.75	7.4	27.8	38	10.6
California oranges.	2 to 3	2.50	11.0	27.5	41	11.3
Sweet potatoes...	2.5 to 3	2.75	8.9	24.5	45	11.0
Peaches	1.5 to 3	2.25	11.9	26.8	45	12.1
Boxed apples ...	1.5 to 3	2.25	10.9	24.7	46	11.4
Cantaloupes	3 to 3.5	3.25	7.6	24.7	46	11.4
Southern cabbage.	2 to 3.5	2.75	9.4	25.9	48	12.4
Barreled apples ..	2.5 to 3.5	3.00	8.0	24.0	49	11.8
Eastern lettuce...	1.5 to 2	1.75	13.0	22.8	51	11.5
Western lettuce..	1 to 2	1.50	14.7	22.1	52	11.6
Yellow onions....	2.5 to 4	3.25	7.1	23.1	53	12.2
Northern cabbage.	3 to 5	4.00	5.2	20.8	58	12.1
White onions	1.5 to 3	2.25	9.0	20.3	63	12.8
Weighted mean.	....	3.28	7.7	25.3	45	11.3

[1] See Appendix Tables, p. 140, for figures and computation of retail and wholesale prices per pound.

[2] Adjusted for shrinkage in retailing.

[3] The decimals are acknowledged to be not precisely accurate, since each of these figures is based on a rounded percentage margin. They are retained for further analysis of jobbers' and retailers' portions.

the product of the value of the standard retail sale and the percentage margin. It is shown in the last column of the table.

The weighted mean value of the standard retail sale for the series is 25.3 cents. It has a range in the commodity series of 7.5 cents, from a minimum of 20.3 cents to a maximum of 27.8 cents. The total range in these values is thus less than one-third of the weighted mean value for the series. It is evident that the *value* of the standard retail sale is

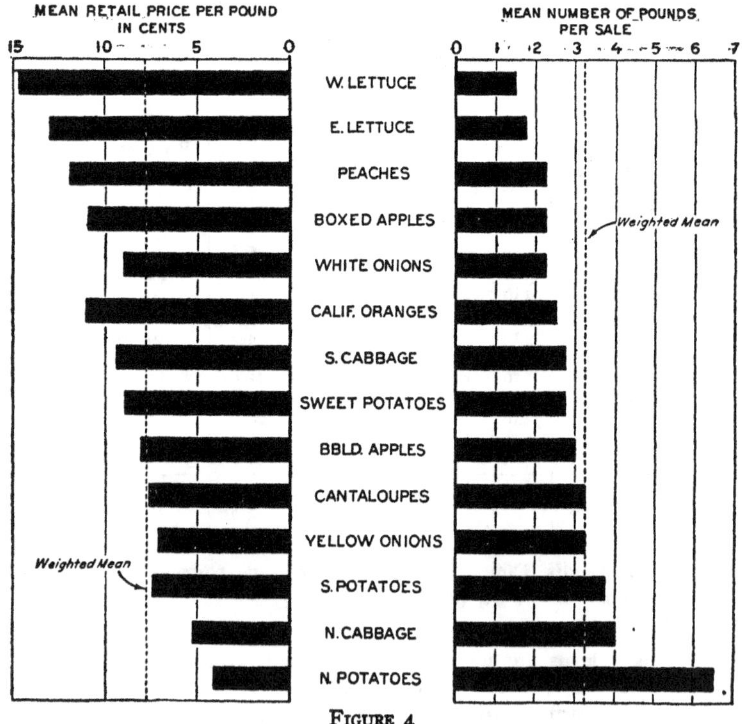

FIGURE 4

decidedly less variable than is the *size* of sale. As shown graphically in Figure 4, variations in size of sale within the series are partially offset by reciprocal variations in price per pound, in such a manner that the variation in their products is materially reduced.

ADEQUACY OF SIZE-OF-SALE TO EXPLAIN MARGIN DIFFERENCES

When the price-spread is expressed in cents per standard retail sale, instead of being expressed as a percentage margin, it is found to have a remarkable degree of uniformity. In the fourteen commodities there is a variation in this spread per sale of less than 3 cents, from a minimum of 9.9 cents to a maximum of 12.8 cents, with a high concentration about the mean for the series. This variation in relation to its mean is much narrower than the variation in the value of the standard sale in relation to its own mean. The price-spread per sale is fairly constant for each article of the series, despite a widely variable size of sale and a considerable variation in the value of the sale. This is shown graphically by the bars in Figure 5.

The commodities with the lower retail value per sale absorb practically the same monetary amount per sale in the distribution process as do the articles with higher value. The wide variation in the percentage margins arises from the uniformity shown in the price-spread per sale and the variability in value of the sale. Within the series of commodities here analysed, the variations in the size of the standard retail sale, in conjunction with the constancy in marketing expense per sale, prove to be an adequate explanation of the margin differences. The amount of money prevailingly expended in the consumer's individual puprchase, coupled with the necessity for a constant spread per sale, fixes the *proportion of the outlay* which is absorbed in distributing the goods.

DEDUCTIONS FROM SIZE-OF-SALE ANALYSIS

This analysis of variations in the margin or distribution expense per dollar's worth, among different perishable com-

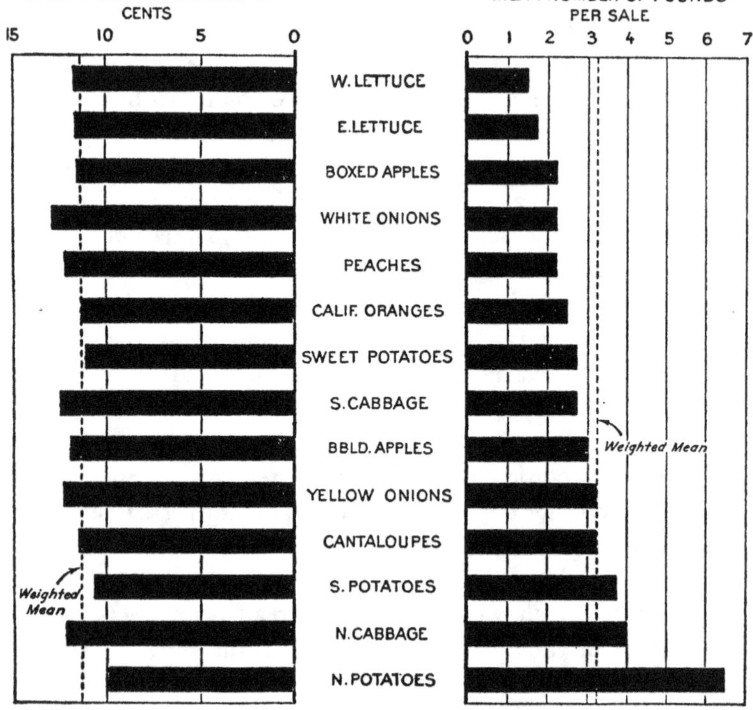

FIGURE 5

modities, demonstrates convincingly that the dominating factor in the variability of percentage margins is the size of the prevailing retail unit of sale. The quantity of goods prevailingly taken at a time by the individual consumer is definitely and regularly associated with the proportion of the consumer's outlay which goes to pay for the services of city distribution.

The percentage margin signifies the amount of money in a retail dollar's worth of goods that is absorbed in these services. The dollar's worth of goods, when expressed in number of sales, is the reciprocal of the value of the retail sale. Thus if the value of the sale is 25 cents, it will require only 4 individual sales to dispose of a dollar's worth of goods, whereas if the value of the sale is 20 cents, 5 sales would be required. Hence, because of the prevailing uniformity in distribution expense for each sale, regardless of its size, the amount absorbed in selling a dollar's worth of goods varies directly with the number of sales which the retailer must make to receive one dollar. As the number of sales increases, the expense for service requirements per dollar likwise increases. The greater the number of sales per dollar, the greater is the proportion of the dollar which is required for distributing the goods; and therefore, the greater is the percentage margin. Differences in margins are thus directly due to differences in size of the retail sale.

The apparently universal practice of marking retail prices so that they will yield a fairly constant monetary spread per retail sale, regardless of the size of sale, thus proves to be so adequate an explanation of the differences in percentage margins in the series of commodities here studied, that it overshadows other factors which might appear to be effective. The effects of such characteristics as the relative total annual volume, total annual value, regularity of supply, perishability, or variability in wholesale price, are of secondary significance because they operate indirectly through price. *The dominating factor is the size and value of the standard retail sale.*

APPORTIONMENT OF PRICE-SPREAD TO JOBBER AND RETAILER

The total spread between wholesale and retail price includes two sorts of distributing services. One set of services is rendered by the distinctive retailing agents, while the other is performed by intermediate jobbers who break up the wholesale shipments into lots of convenient size for handling by retailers. In order to ascertain the relation which these two portions of the total price-spread bear to each other, the spread per retail sale was split up into its two component parts. The portion attributable to the retailer was measured separately from that of the jobber. This analysis was restricted to independent unit stores, since in chain stores the functions of jobber and retailer are performed by a single agency. The retailers' portion of the price-spread is the difference between the retail price and the jobbing price; while the jobber's portion is the difference between the jobbers' selling price and the price of goods in the New York wholesale market.

The retailers' portion and the jobbers' portion of the total price-spread in unit stores, and the value of the standard retail sale are shown for each commodity in Table 13. Comparison of these two portions shows that the retailer's part of the distribution expense is much more nearly constant throughout the commodity series than is the jobber's portion. The deviation of the jobbers' price-spread from its mean for the fourteen articles is over twice as great as the deviation of the retailers' price-spread from its mean. The mean jobbers' spread for the series is 2.1 cents per retail sale, and the coefficient of deviation from the mean is 18 per cent of the mean. The mean retailers' spread for the series is 9.7 cents per sale and the coefficient of deviation from this mean is only 8 per cent of the mean.

Comparison of jobbers' spreads and retailers' spreads shows that there is no regularity of association between the

TABLE 13

RETAILERS' AND JOBBERS' PORTION IN STANDARD RETAIL SALE FOR UNIT STORES ONLY. NEW YORK METROPOLITAN AREA, FEBRUARY, 1923–MAY, 1924

Commodity	Value of standard retail sale	Total spread	Jobbers' spread	Retailers' spread
	Cents	Cents	Cents	Cents
California oranges	28.0	11.8	2.0	9.8
Southern potatoes	27.8	10.8	1.6	9.2
Northern potatoes	27.3	10.4	1.7	8.7
Peaches	27.0	12.2	2.5	9.7
Southern cabbage	26.4	12.7	2.9	9.8
Sweet potatoes	25.9	11.9	1.8	10.1
Boxed apples	25.2	11.8	2.7	9.1
Cantaloupes	24.7	11.6	2.0	9.6
Barreled apples	24.6	12.3	2.0	10.3
Eastern lettuce	23.5	12.2	3.0	9.2
Yellow onions	23.4	12.4	1.6	10.8
Western lettuce	22.4	11.9	1.8	10.1
Northern cabbage	21.6	12.5	1.9	10.6
White onions	20.9	13.4	2.5	10.9
14-commodity weighted mean	25.9	11.8	2.1	9.7

two. It is the constancy in distribution service rendered per sale by the retailer which accounts for the uniformity in total spread throughout the commodity series. The retailer's service is thus the dominant factor in determining the expense of distribution.

The bar chart in Figure 6 shows graphically for each article the split-up of the standard retail sale into its three component parts. The dark portion at the left of each bar represents the wholesale value of the goods sold, while the middle part indicates the portion required for jobbers' service, and the right-hand section represents the amount required by the retailer. The chart emphasizes the general uniformity of the retailers' portion, and the relative variability of the jobbers' portion.

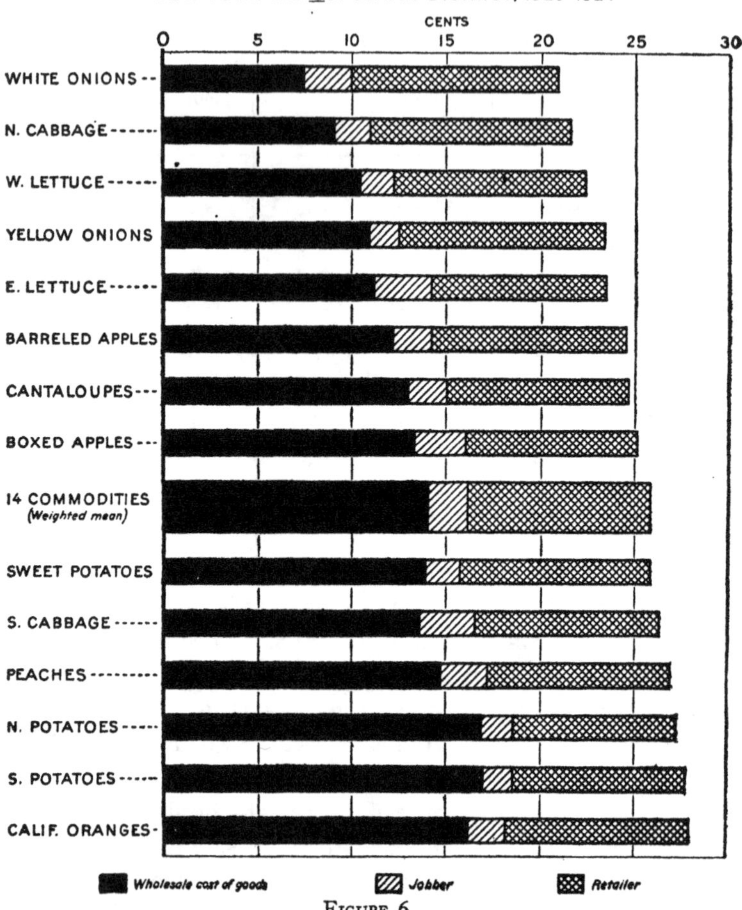

FIGURE 6

VARIABILITY OF JOBBERS' PORTION OF STANDARD RETAIL SALE

It was suggested that the considerable variability in the jobbers' spreads in the standard retail sale might be explained by showing their association with variations in the prevailing *size of jobber's sale,* in a manner similar to the explanation of variability in percentage margins. To test the existence of such association, the prevailing size of the jobber's sale was ascertained for each commodity, and this was compared with the size of the retail sale. The figures for size of the jobber's sale were obtained from the books of representative jobbers in Brooklyn and Newark, covering transactions of several weeks.

TABLE 14

RELATION BETWEEN SIZE OF JOBBER'S SALE AND SIZE OF RETAILER'S SALE. NEW YORK METROPOLITAN AREA, FEBRUARY, 1923–MAY, 1924

Commodity	Mean number of pounds per jobber's sale	Mean number of pounds per retailer's sale	Number of retail sales per jobber's sale [1]
	Pounds	Pounds	Sales
Eastern lettuce	54	1.75	31
Western lettuce	58	1.50	39
Peaches	65	2.25	28
Sweet potatoes	75	2.75	24
Boxed apples	80	2.25	35
California oranges	84	2.50	34
Southern cabbage	95	2.75	31
Cantaloupes	96	3.25	30
Barreled apples	100	3.06	30
White onions	100	2.25	43
Yellow onions	110	3.25	32
Northern cabbage	125	4.00	28
Southern potatoes	183	3.75	45
Northern potatoes	225	6.50	33
Weighted mean	112	3.28	32.5

Relationship between the size of jobber's sale and the size of the standard retail sale was found to be substantially regular throughout the series, as shown in Table 14. Among the fourteen articles the range in the number of retail sales per jobber's sale is from a minimum of 24 to a maximum of

[1] Allowing for shrinkage in retail selling according to Table 9.

45 sales, but the grouping around their weighted mean number is fairly close. Moreover, eight of the commodities have a ratio lying between 30 and 35; for three of the remaining six it is below 30, and with the remaining three it is above 35. A general tendency is thus apparent for the size of the jobber's sale to vary directly with the size of the retailer's sale, as is shown graphically in Figure 7.

Since general regularity exists in the association of size of jobber's sale with size of retail sale, and since there is also

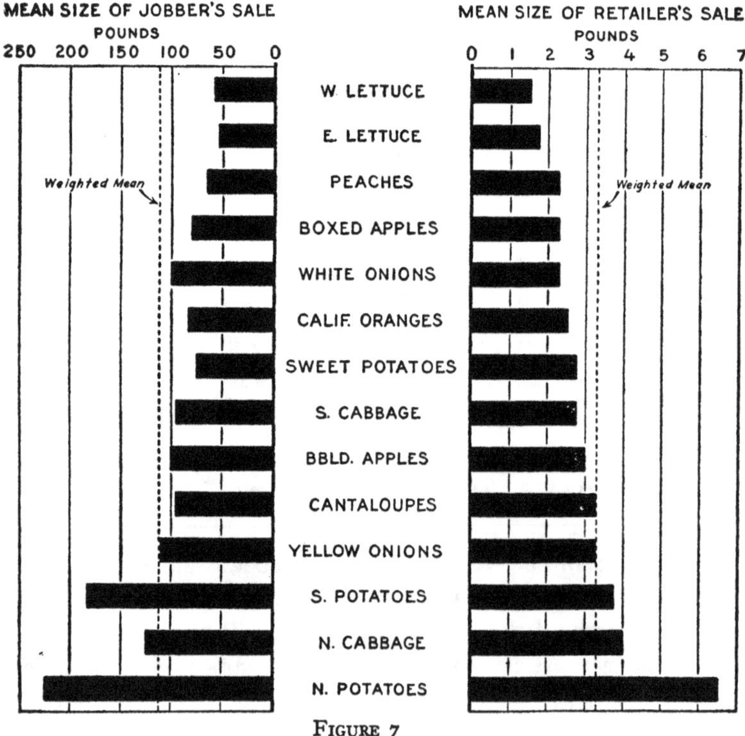

FIGURE 7

lack of association between jobbers' spreads and retailers' spreads, it is not possible to explain variations in jobbers' spreads by the variability in size of the jobber's sale.

RELATION OF JOBBERS' SPREADS TO WHOLESALE PRICE CHANGES

Speculative risks in varying degrees are incurred by jobbers because of price fluctuations in the wholesale market. Commodities which suffer wide or sudden price changes give greater opportunity for monetary loss than articles whose prices are fairly stable. The risks arising from such price variations might with some reason be expected to influence the selling policies of dealers in the jobbing market, and thus to account for variability in jobbers' price-spreads for different kinds of commodities. Tests were therefore made to ascertain if there was any regular association between the jobbers' portion in the standard retail sale and variability in wholesale price.

A measure of variation is required which will avoid the effects of pronounced seasonal price trends. The usual measures of dispersion, such as the average deviation and standard deviation, are unsatisfactory for this purpose. An adequate quantitative measure is required to indicate comparable price changes in the variable seasons when different articles are in the market. For this purpose, the wholesale price of each commodity was taken for an identical day in each week of the season in which it was officially reported in the New York market. Prices for Thursday of each week were taken from the Daily Market Report of the United States Department of Agriculture.[1] The average week-to-week change in price, either up or down, was determined and expressed as a percentage of the season's mean wholesale

[1] Wholesale prices for California oranges were obtained from the *Daily Fruit Reporter*.

price for the given commodity. This percentage is an accurate measure of tendency-to-change in wholesale price, which may be used as an index for comparing the different articles. The price variability of eastern lettuce, for example, is shown by its index of 26.4 per cent, to be very much greater than that of northern potatoes, whose index is 3.2 per cent. These indices mean that the average week-to-week change in wholesale price throughout the market season for lettuce is 26.4 per cent of the mean price for the lettuce season; whereas for potatoes the mean week-to-week change in wholesale price is only 3.2 per cent of the average price for the potato season.

The index of variability in wholesale price for each article in the series [1] is shown in Table 15 and Figure 8. Naturally a wide range exists in the indices. The commodities fall

TABLE 15

INDEX OF VARIABILITY IN WHOLESALE PRICES, NEW YORK METROPOLITAN AREA, FEBRUARY, 1923–MAY, 1924 [1]

Low		Medium		High	
	Per cent		Per cent		Per cent
Northern potatoes..	3.2	Southern potatoes ..	11.8	Western lettuce....	19.6
Boxed apples	4.6	Northern cabbage ..	12.8	Cantaloupes	22.8
Sweet potatoes	5.4	Yellow onions	13.5	Peaches	24.1
Barreled apples	8.0			Southern cabbage..	25.9
California oranges..	9.2			Eastern lettuce	26.4

quite definitely into three distinct groups, having low, medium, and high variability respectively. Five of the articles have a distinctly low index,—less than 10 per cent. Three commodities are in a medium group, with indices between 10 per cent and 15 per cent. In the remaining five articles there is high variability, near or above 20 per cent.

[1] White onions are omitted because of lack of continuous price quotations.

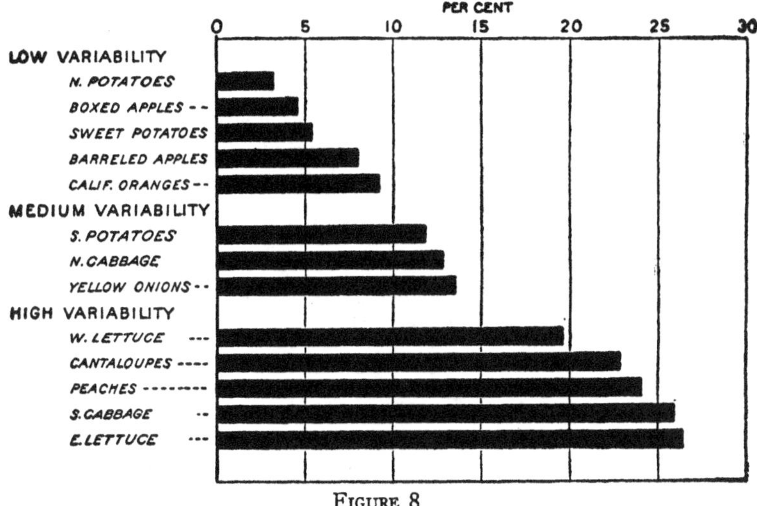

FIGURE 8

This grouping of the commodities according to variability in wholesale price agrees in general with their relative perishability. The low-variability group includes the more staple articles which keep fairly well. These may be supplied to the market or withheld from it according to its demands, so that the variation between supply and demand is kept fairly uniform throughout the season. In the high-variability group, on the other hand, are the distinctly seasonal articles, with limited keeping qualities. They must be shipped from the producing areas as soon as ready for market, and they are thrown upon the market immediately after arrival. Consequently, because the erratic seasonal changes in supply are not balanced by corresponding adjustment in consumer's demand, they suffer wide fluctuations in wholesale price.

[1] White onions omitted because of lack of continuous price quotations.

Is there any regular association in the three groups between the index of wholesale price variability and the jobbers' spread in the retail sale? Apparently not, judging from comparison of the two columns in Table 16. Two of the commodities whose spread per sale is lowest are in the middle variability group. Boxed apples, which have a high price-spread, are in the low variability group; and three other articles, which also have a high price-spread per sale, are in the high variability group. From the data on which these comparisons are based, there appears to be no regularity of association between variability of wholesale prices and the portion of the consumer's outlay required for jobbers' services. The results of the comparisons are generally negative.

TABLE 16

RELATION OF JOBBERS' PRICE-SPREAD TO WHOLESALE PRICE VARIABILITY. NEW YORK METROPOLITAN AREA, FEBRUARY, 1923–MAY, 1924

Commodity	Jobbers' spread per retail sale	Wholesale price variability
	Cents	Per cent
Yellow onions	1.6	13.5
Southern potatoes	1.6	11.8
Northern potatoes	1.7	3.2
Sweet potatoes	1.8	5.4
Western lettuce	1.8	19.6
Northern cabbage	1.9	12.8
Cantaloupes	2.0	22.8
California oranges	2.0	9.2
Barreled apples	2.0	8.0
Peaches	2.5	24.1
Boxed apples	2.7	4.6
Southern cabbage	2.9	25.9
Western lettuce	3.0	26.4

Variability in jobbers' spread is not accounted for by variations in size of jobber's sale. Neither does variability in the jobbers' portion of the price-spread appear to be associated with variations of price in the wholesale market. It must be accounted for by factors outside of those considered here.

CHAPTER V

Store-Operation Contrasts

The present analysis is concerned with measurement of the influence of some typical forms of store operation in the city distribution of perishables.

CLASSIFICATION OF STORE TYPES [1]

For the purpose of determining the extent to which the factor of management and the factor of service policy influence the expense of distribution and the cost of goods to consumers, two classifications of store-types are here considered. Under the first classification, based on the kind of management, all retail stores are divided into two main groups: (1) unit stores under independent operation by individual proprietors, and (2) chain stores operated as parts of centrally organized systems. In the other classification, stores are distinguished on the basis of the special services they render. The service distinctions apply to unit stores only, dividing them into three general groups. The first service group contains unit stores whose regular policy is to extend credit and to deliver orders to a majority of their customers. The second group includes stores which operate prevailingly on a cash basis, but grant a limited amount of delivery service. The third group comprises unit stores which operate on a strict cash-and-carry basis, extending neither credit nor delivery. No stores of a credit-carry type were represented in the data. Subdivisions of chain store

[1] Characteristics of the various types of retail stores are discussed in chap. ii, pp. 24-30.

data were not attempted on the basis of service, since the price averages in all reporting chain stores were nearly identical with those of the prevailing cash-carry type.[1]

Distinctions between independent retail stores as to class of trade or clientele, coincide generally with distinctions on the basis of service rendered. The more discriminating high-class trade of well-to-do neighborhoods is generally served by stores operating on a full credit-and-delivery basis. Many independent retailers in thrifty middle-class neighborhoods conduct their business on a cash basis, but render a limited amount of delivery service to their regular customers. The poorer and middle-class neighborhoods where low prices are the main consideration, are served mainly by cash-and-carry stores, which dispense entirely with credit and delivery services. Chain stores do an extensive business in the low-price sections also.

Although the original data of unit stores were carefully tabulated on the basis of specialization, as grocery stores and fruit-vegetable stores,[2] the slight contrasts found in the distribution expense of these two groups indicated that specialization is a factor of less significance than the factors of management and service. Further study of the influence of specialization was therefore discontinued, in order that attention might be concentrated upon the more influential factors. The present analysis thus takes into consideration the distinctions between five types of retailing agencies,

[1] See Appendix, pp. 154-9.

[2] See store-type comparisons (grocery and fruit-vegetable unit stores) in Appendix, p. 150. The differences there noted in the weighted mean spread per car for the 14-commodity series shows an advantage of $110 in favor of the fruit-vegetable specialist. This difference is divided equally between retailer and jobber. Inspection of the figures from which the weighted means are computed shows that although the total spread is generally lower in the fruit-vegetable stores the split-up has no regularity among the individual commodities.

classified in two categories according to their form of management and extent of service, thus:

Management	*Service-policy (Unit stores only)*
Unit stores [1]	Credit-delivery
Chain stores	Cash-delivery
	Cash-carry

EXTENT AND ADJUSTMENT OF DATA

The data for only seven of the fourteen commodities previously considered were used in these store-type analyses. The insufficient number of quotations in some store-groups prevented making valid comparisons for the other commodities. Nearly three-fourths of the original number of quotations [2] are included, however, in the seven commodities retained. These comprise 68 per cent of the total annual volume of the larger series, and 70 per cent of their total annual retail value. Moreover the weighted mean percentage margins for these seven articles are practically the same as those for the complete series.[3] The smaller number of articles may therefore be regarded as representative of the larger series of fruits and vegetables.

To make entirely valid comparisons of results from the various groups of data, it was necessary to adjust retail prices to allow for certain discrepancies occurring in the original wholesale prices. These irregularities arose from lack of identity in dates of quotations, or from variability in grades of goods reported by different store-types.

[1] In the subsequent comparisons, the all-unit, or typical unit store figures are regarded as representing the degree of service generally prevailing in metropolitan unit stores. The typical unit store is thus to be considered as a composite, rather than an actual type, since the figures were based upon the averages of the original quotations, which were secured from stores with all three types of service-policy.

[2] See Appendix, p. 153.

[3] See Appendix, p. 159.

To accomplish the adjustment, a weighted average wholesale price per car was computed for the seven commodities as a common base for the five store-types, by giving chain stores and unit stores the respective weights of 1 and 9, according to their relative importance as metropolitan distributors.[1] With this weighted average figure as a base, an adjusted retail price for each store group was then constructed by adding to this the same spread as existed between the original wholesale and retail figures. The spreads between the weighted average wholesale prices and the adjusted retail prices per car remain the same as before adjustment, but retail prices now reflect only the contrasts due to variations in type of store. The weighted average wholesale price for the seven commodity series is $1180 per car. In Table 17 are given the figures for the original wholesale and retail prices, with the spread in each of the five store groups. The same figures after adjustment, based upon the uniform wholesale figure of $1180 per car, are given in Table 18. The spread in this table for each store type is identical with

TABLE 17

ORIGINAL (UNADJUSTED) WHOLESALE AND RETAIL PRICES, AND PRICE-SPREAD PER CAR IN FIVE STORE-TYPES. 7 COMMODITY WEIGHTED AVERAGES, NEW YORK METROPOLITAN AREA, FEBRUARY, 1923–MAY, 1924

Store-type	Wholesale Price	Retail Price	Price Spread
	Dollars	Dollars	Dollars
Chain	1130	1700	570
All unit	1185	2180	995
Cash-carry	1135	1960	825
Cash-delivery	1190	2095	905
Credit-delivery	1200	2275	1075

[1] See chap. i, p. 25.

that derived from the original prices. The price-spread for each of the seven commodities in the five store groups is shown in Table 19.

TABLE 18

ADJUSTED WHOLESALE AND RETAIL PRICES AND PRICE-SPREAD PER CAR IN FIVE STORE-TYPES. 7 COMMODITY WEIGHTED AVERAGES, NEW YORK METROPOLITAN AREA, FEBRUARY, 1923–MAY, 1924

Store-type	Wholesale Price	Retail Price	Price Spread
	Dollars	Dollars	Dollars
Chain	1180	1750	570
All unit	1180	2175	995
Cash-carry	1180	2005	825
Cash-delivery	1180	2085	905
Credit-delivery	1180	2255	1075

TABLE 19

PRICE-SPREAD PER CAR FOR EACH COMMODITY IN FIVE STORE-TYPES, NEW YORK METROPOLITAN AREA, FEBRUARY, 1923–MAY, 1924

Commodity	Chain stores	All unit stores	Cash-carry stores	Cash-delivery stores	Credit-delivery stores
	Dollars	Dollars	Dollars	Dollars	Dollars
Northern potatoes	210	615	600	580	645
California oranges	870	1465	985	1260	1635
Sweet potatoes	330	880	470	815	990
Boxed apples	1010	1575	1340	1445	1685
Barreled apples	570	960	830	880	1045
Eastern lettuce	695	940	885	845	990
Yellow onions	675	905	745	870	970
Weighted mean	570	995	825	905	1075

MANNER OF MAKING COMPARISONS

The relative advantage of each of the five forms of store operation in the distribution of the typical commodities is indicated by the contrasts or differentials in their respective retail prices and in their price-spreads. These differentials are presented in two forms. The first form shows contrasts in the expense of distribution as represented by the spread between wholesale price and retail price in each of the five types of store. These differentials in cost of distribution are primarily of interest to dealers and other food-handling agencies which deal in large quantities of goods. The contrasts are therefore presented on a per-car basis, in terms of *dollars per car.* The second form shows the contrasts between different store-types in retail selling prices. Since to the individual consumer the final retail prices rather than the intermediate handling costs are of primary interest, the price differentials of the various store-types are expressed in *cents per standard retail sale,* the unit which is of direct concern to the consuming public.

DIFFERENTIALS IN DISTRIBUTION EXPENSE

The differentials in price-spreads of the respective store types represent their contrasts in city distribution expense, and thus indicate the relative advantage of each type as a distributing agency. In Table 20 are shown the management differentials between chain stores and unit stores, in terms of dollars per car and also as percentages of the respective unit-store spreads, for each commodity and as weighted averages for the whole group. These indicate the contrasts between the chain store and the typical unit store, and between the chain store and the cash-and-carry unit store.

Between the typical unit store and the chain store there is observed an average gross difference for the 7-commodity group amounting to $425 per car, in favor of the chain-store form of management. This is approximately 43 per cent below the average price-spread found in the typical unit

TABLE 20. MANAGEMENT DIFFERENCES: COMPARISON OF PRICE-SPREADS IN CHAIN STORES AND UNIT STORES, NEW YORK METROPOLITAN AREA, FEBRUARY, 1923–MAY, 1924

Commodity	Price-Spreads			Differentials in Price-Spreads			
	Chain-store	Typical-unit-store	Cash-carry unit store	Gross differential: between typical unit store and chain store		Net differential: between cash-carry unit store and chain store	
	Dollars per car	Dollars per car	Dollars per car	Dollars per car	Percentage of typical-unit-store spread	Dollars per car	Percentage of cash-carry-unit store spread
7-commodity mean (weighted according to annual volumes)	$570	$995	$825	$425	42.7%	$255	30.9%
Northern potatoes	210	615	600	405	65.8	390	65.0
California oranges	870	1465	985	595	40.6	115	11.7
Sweet potatoes	330	880	470	550	62.5	140	29.8
Boxed apples	1010	1575	1340	565	35.9	330	24.6
Barreled apples	570	960	830	390	40.6	260	31.3
Eastern lettuce	695	940	885	245	26.0	190	21.5
Yellow onions	675	905	745	230	25.4	70	9.3

store. In other words, the figures indicate that city distribution expenses in chain stores averaged 43 per cent below the expenses in typical unit stores. When the two types of management are compared on an identical non-service basis, the contrast in favor of the chain store is reduced to $225 per car, which is 31 per cent below the distribution expense in cash-and-carry unit stores. These latter comparisons are truer measures of the difference due solely to the form of management, since in the first comparisons there was some difference in the service rendered. Certain reservations must be kept in mind, however, in interpreting these contrasts which are so favorable to chain stores, lest unwarranted conclusions be hastily drawn. These reservations are necessary to give correct meaning to the results of the analysis.

It should be borne in mind first that the basic figures for the wholesale prices which were used in computing price-spreads were the official quotations in the New York wholesale market.[1] With independent retailers who actually depend upon city marketing agencies for their supplies of perishables, the prices prevailing in the wholesale market do fix the actual city wholesale cost of their goods. Hence the above price-spreads for unit stores represent actual city distribution expense in the metropolitan area. In the case of chain stores, however, this is not universally true. As a matter of fact, a considerable part of the fruits and vegetables sold by leading chain-store systems do not pass through the New York wholesale market at all. This is especially true of potatoes, which are often purchased in carload lots and even in trainloads from local shippers in the producing agricultural sections. To a considerable extent this is true also of onions, lettuce and apples, and of other commodities in the height of their season. With oranges, on the other hand, which are wholesaled mainly through the fruit auctions,

[1] See chap. iii, p. 55.

both chain stores and independents must obtain supplies through the same New York marketing channels. Therefore chain stores do not enjoy a great advantage over unit stores in purchasing this commodity, and it is observed that the price-spreads for California oranges are not widely divergent in the two management types.

The consequence of such large-scale buying outside of the city market is that the wholesaler is eliminated and that his functions are combined with those of the retailing agency. Of course this does not eliminate the wholesaling expense, but it enables chain stores to make certain economies through direct shipment and reduction of intermediate handling. The lower price-spread of chain stores shown above is thus due in part to certain economies external to city distribution. This is true particularly of commodities wherein chain-store methods of purchase differ widely from the methods of independent stores. To present an exact statement of the total expense of city distribution in chain stores, it would be necessary to add to their apparent price-spreads as given above the difference between the actual cost of their goods on arrival in New York and the prices in the New York wholesale market.

Contrasts in the method of purchasing other articles within the city marketing system have a similar bearing upon the differences in price-spreads. The large chain-store systems do not generally depend upon the jobbing markets, but they purchase their supplies directly in the city wholesale market, thus taking over the jobber's functions into their own hands. Here, however, the spread between original cost and retail price does not include any element external to city distribution. Hence comparison of chain stores with unit stores, for commodities purchased by each type wholly within the city marketing system, is fully valid, for their differences arise wholly from differences in methods of city distribution.

The wide contrast in favor of chain stores shown in Table 20 is probably accounted for in large measure by the chain-store policy of advertising and selling certain articles as " leaders ", for the purpose of drawing grocery trade. Executives of chain-store systems have stated that the original purpose in adding fruits and vegetables to their stocks was primarily to attract grocery customers. Expectation of profit from perishables was a secondary consideration. Even now the majority of chain stores carry only the more staple perishables and seasonal articles, although generally the variety has been increased somewhat in recent years. The large chain-store systems use potatoes frankly as a " leader ". This commodity is particularly advantageous for such sale because of its general use by all customers, and because of the economies to be gained through purchasing and handling in quantity. The chain-store prices for potatoes are frequently so close to the wholesale price that independent retailers make no attempt to compete.

It is observed that potatoes tower above all the other commodities in the percentage differential between the chain-store spread and the unit-store spread. This commodity exerts a dominating influence in the weighted average for the seven-commodity group, because potatoes comprise nearly one-third (29 per cent) of the total annual volume of the series. Sweet potatoes, whose percentage differential in the typical unit store is also high, exert a minor influence, as this commodity comprises only 5 per cent of the total annual volume. The prevailing use of potatoes as leaders by chain stores, together with the practice of purchasing this commodity outside of the New York market, thus explains to a considerable degree the wide divergence of price-spreads in favor of chain-store management.

Another consideration apart from method of store operation should also be borne in mind in interpreting the apparent chain-store advantage. This has to do with the particular data used for analysis. Selling prices of chain stores are fairly standardized for individual commodities in all the metropolitan units of a given system. Chain stores make their appeal largely on a price basis, and they make a feature of uniform prices. Independent retailers, on the other hand, have no such standard price policy. Those which appeal to higher-class trade do so on the basis either of quality or of service. Thus even cash-and-carry unit stores may emphasize extra quality or freshness of goods, and base their prices accordingly. Such unit stores differ widely among themselves in the range of goods and in freedom of choice, as well as in general quality. Consequently independent stores have no such price uniformity as exists in chain stores, either in different sections or within a given locality, because of the the variable classes of trade and the differing merchandizing policies of individual retailers. Chain stores are much more nearly uniform in regard to qualities of goods, as well as in their clientele and in service policies. Hence in a comparison of price data collected from miscellaneous unit stores and fairly homogeneous chain stores, the variability of the former tends to increase their average price-spread.

The conclusions as to the actual chain-store advantage in management are thus modified by two important qualifications: (1) by the extent of advantage obtained by purchasing supplies outside of the New York market, and (2) by the extent to which perishables fail to bear their proportionate share of general store-operation expense. It is necessary to take these two factors into account to ascertain the true management differential in favor of chain stores.

Comparisons of price-spread in independent unit stores, based upon distinctions in service policy, are given in Table 21. It is observed that the average differential in price-spread between the credit-delivery type and the cash-carry

TABLE 21. SERVICE DIFFERENCES: COMPARISONS OF PRICE-SPREADS IN DIFFERENT TYPES OF UNIT STORES, NEW YORK METROPOLITAN AREA, FEBRUARY, 1923–MAY, 1924

Commodity	Price-Spreads			Differentials in Price-Spreads Between			
	Cash-carry	Cash-delivery	Credit-delivery	Cash-delivery and cash-carry	Credit-delivery and cash-delivery	Credit-delivery and cash-carry	
	Dollars per car	Dollars per car	Dollars per car	Dollars per car	Dollars per car	Dollars per car	Percentage of credit-delivery spread
7-commodity mean (weighted according to annual volumes)	$825	$905	$1075	$80	$170	$250	23.2%
Northern potatoes	600	580	645	—20	65	45	6.9
California oranges	985	1260	1635	275	375	650	39.7
Sweet potatoes	470	815	990	345	175	520	52.5
Boxed apples	1340	1445	1685	105	240	345	20.4
Barreled apples	830	880	1045	50	165	215	20.5
Eastern lettuce	885	845	990	—40	145	105	10.6
Yellow onions	745	870	970	125	100	225	23.1

type is $250 per car. This means that the average price-spread of cash-carry stores was about 23 per cent below the average for credit-delivery stores. In other words, nearly one-fourth of the distribution expense in the credit-delivery

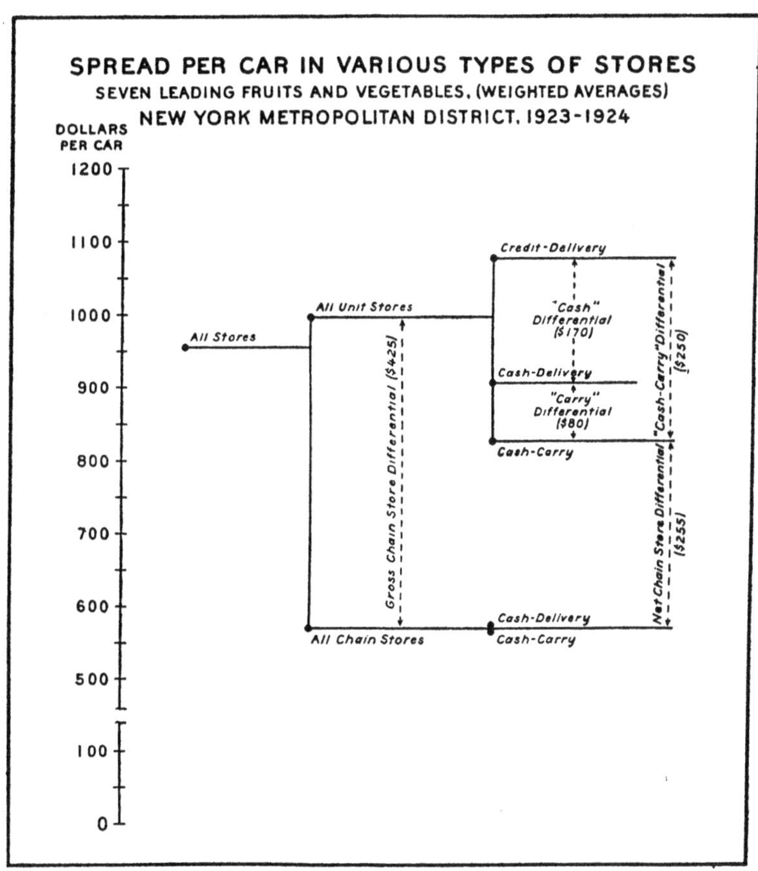

FIGURE 9

type is accounted for by the expense of delivery and the granting of credit. Northern potatoes and eastern lettuce show relatively slight divergence in the two contrasted types, while great divergence is shown by sweet potatoes and California oranges.

A graphic summary of the differences in distribution expense per car, among the different types of management and service, is presented in Figure 9.

DIFFERENCES IN PRICES TO CONSUMERS

To the individual consumer the significance of the contrasts in store types is more obvious when they are expressed as differences in retail prices for small quantities. The value of the standard retail sale is here used as the unit of comparison. The values for each of the seven commodities in each of the five store-types, are given in Table 22, with the weighted mean for the series, as computed from the classified retail price data and from the size-of-sale data. The values are thus uncompensated for adjustments in the wholesale price differences.

TABLE 22

VALUE OF STANDARD RETAIL SALE,[1] IN DIFFERENT STORE-TYPES, NEW YORK METROPOLITAN AREA, FEBRUARY, 1923–MAY, 1924

Commodity	Chain stores	All unit stores	Cash-carry stores	Cash-delivery stores	Credit-delivery stores
	Cents	Cents	Cents	Cents	Cents
Northern potatoes	19.9	27.7	26.0	27.4	28.2
California oranges	23.8	28.1	24.2	26.3	29.7
Sweet potatoes	16.5	25.9	18.2	23.8	27.6
Boxed apples	19.5	25.4	22.9	24.3	26.4
Barreled apples	19.1	24.6	22.1	23.7	25.8
Eastern lettuce	18.4	23.4	22.8	22.1	24.6
Yellow onions	20.4	23.5	21.2	23.4	24.4
Weighted mean	20.2	25.9	23.3	24.9	27.0

[1] Unadjusted for wholesale price differences.

When retail prices are compensated for the wholesale differences noted in Table 17, the differentials in the value of the retail sale for the various store-types are synonymous with the original differentials in price-spread per retail sale. For convenience in computation, therefore, the original price-spreads per car were employed here. By dividing the per-car figure for each commodity by the number of retail sales per car,[1] the real spread in value of the retail sale is derived for the various store groups. The average price-spread for the seven-commodity series was obtained by dividing the per-car figure by 8405, the weighted mean number of retail sales per car.

The differentials in value of the retail sale among the five store groups, for each commodity and for the commodity series as a whole, are presented in Table 23. In the last column the average differentials are given also as percentages of the retail prices in the respective store-types.

The percentage differentials among store types are much smaller proportionally than are the differentials in price-spreads, because here the basis of comparison is the *retail price,* whereas the former comparisons were based upon *spread* between retail and wholesale prices. Between the chain store and the typical unit store there was found a gross difference of 5 cents per standard retail sale. Retail prices in chain stores thus averaged 17 per cent below those obtaining in typical unit stores which gave the prevailing amount of special service. When the (cash-and-carry) chain store is compared with the cash-and-carry unit store, both types being on the same non-service basis, the net difference in retail prices in favor of the chain store is reduced to 3 cents per sale, which is 13 per cent below the cash-carry unit store price. Here again the latter figure of 13 per cent is a truer measure of the real advantage of chain-store man-

[1] See Appendix, p. 160.

TABLE 23. MANAGEMENT AND SERVICE DIFFERENTIALS AMONG FIVE-STORE TYPES, IN VALUE OF THE STANDARD RETAIL SALE, NEW YORK METROPOLITAN AREA, FEBRUARY, 1923–MAY, 1924

Types of store operation compared	Differentials per retail sale [1]								
	Northern potatoes	California oranges	Sweet potatoes	Boxed apples	Barreled apples	Eastern lettuce	Yellow onions	7-commodity weighted mean	Mean percentage of retail price [2]
	Cents	Cents	Cents	Cents	Cents	Cents	Cents	Cents	Per cent
Management: chain store and unit store:									
Gross chain-store decrease below typical unit store	7.0	4.8	7.5	4.3	5.0	3.2	3.2	5.0	17
Net chain-store decrease below cash-carry unit store	6.7	0.9	1.9	2.5	3.3	2.4	1.0	3.0	13
Service: different unit store types:									
Cash-carry decrease below credit-delivery	0.8	5.2	7.1	2.6	2.7	1.4	3.1	3.0	11
Cash-delivery decrease below credit-delivery	1.1	3.0	2.4	1.8	2.1	1.9	1.4	2.0	8
Cash-carry decrease below cash-delivery	—0.3	2.2	4.7	0.8	0.6	—0.5	1.7	1.0	4

[1] Adjusted for wholesale price differences.

[2] These percentages are rounded, hence the last three do not agree exactly.

agement, since the former larger percentage difference contained some contrast in service.

When unit stores are compared according to their respec-

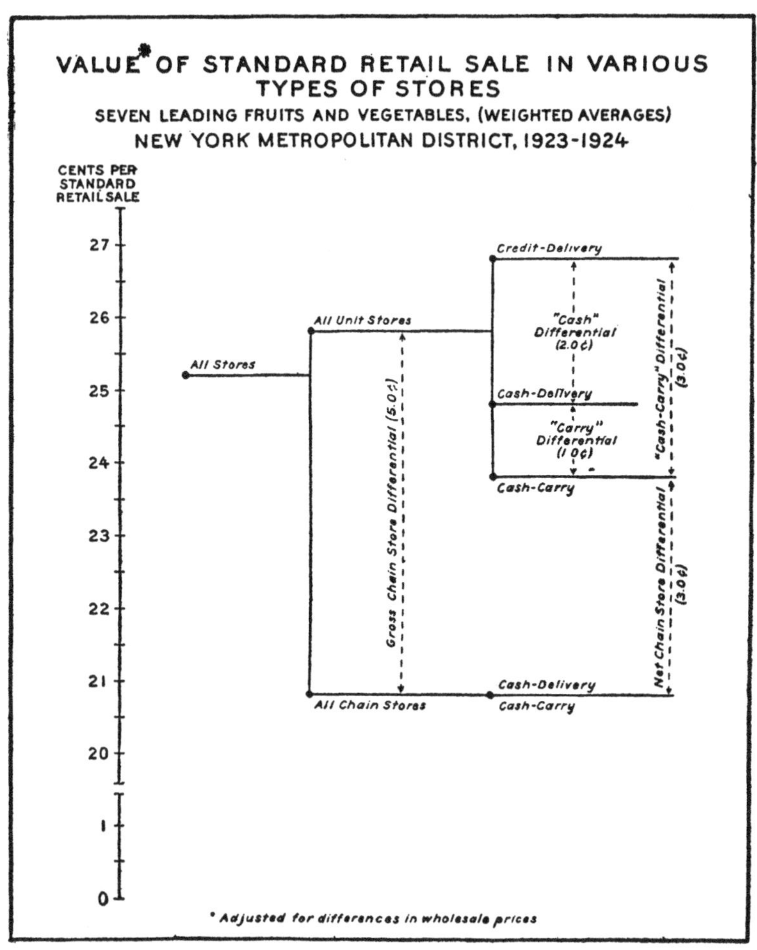

FIGURE 10

tive service policies, credit-and-delivery service together are found to have cost the consumer an average of 3 cents per retail sale, in contrast to prices of cash-carry unit stores. This service differential is 11 per cent of the retail price in the full-service type of store. From the data from which these differences were derived, the credit element accounts for a greater proportion than does the delivery element. This result may be due in a measure to the limited extent of delivery service granted by the reporting stores of the cash-and-delivery group.

A graphic summary of the average differences in price to consumers among the five types of management and service, in terms of the value of the standard retail sale, is given in Figure 10.

The differences found in this analysis of management and service factors, showing the split-up of the consumer's outlay per standard sale in the various forms of store operation, are shown in fuller detail in Figure 11. Here the dark portion at the left of each bar represents the wholesale cost of the goods disposed of in the standard retail sale. This wholesale portion,—14 cents—is made uniform for each type. The remaining part of each bar shows the distribution expense for services. In the chain store, all distribution services were rendered at a total expense of 6.8 cents per sale. In the unit-store types there was added a charge for jobber's service of 2 cents per sale. The general retailer's services in the cash-carry unit store cost 7.8 cents. Total distribution expense for retailer and jobber in the cash-carry unit store was thus 3 cents per sale greater than in the chain store. In the unit store which operated on a cash basis with limited delivery service, the expense of delivery added 1 cent more. In the type which granted credit in addition to delivery, 2 cents more were required to cover the expense of credit service.

SPLIT-UP OF CONSUMER'S OUTLAY* IN VARIOUS TYPES OF STORES.
(PER STANDARD RETAIL SALE)
SEVEN LEADING FRUITS AND VEGETABLES, (WEIGHTED AVERAGES)
NEW YORK METROPOLITAN DISTRICT, 1923-1924
CENTS
TOTAL CONSUMER'S OUTLAY CENTS
0 5 10 15 20 25 30
GOODS
SERVICES
CHAIN STORES 20.8
14
ALL SERVICES 6.8
UNIT CASH-CARRY STORES 23.8
14 2 7.8
UNIT CASH DELIVERY STORES 24.8
14 2 1
UNIT CREDIT DELIVERY STORES 26.8
14 2 1 2
GOODS
Wholesale cost of Goods 14 Cents
SERVICES
Jobbers Service 2 Cents
General Retailers Service 7.8 Cents
Delivery 1 Cent
Credit 2 Cents
*Adjusted for differences in wholesale prices

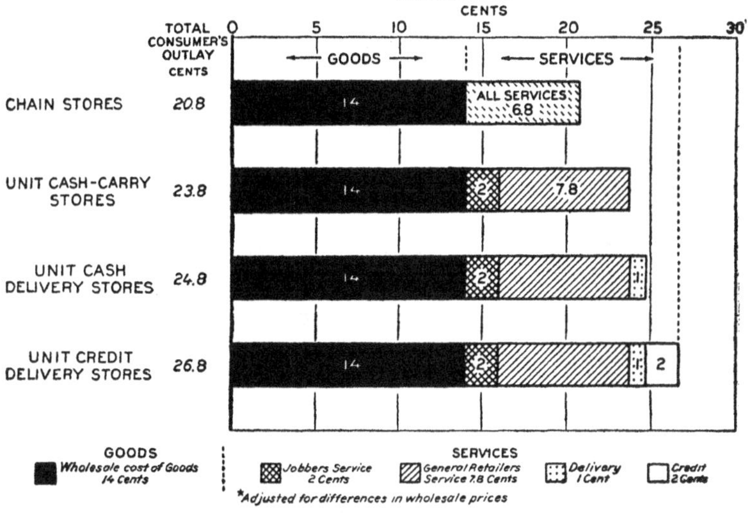

FIGURE II

CHAPTER VI

Implications of Commodity Contrasts

In the early consideration of factors regarded as having a possible bearing upon the contrasts in distribution expense in the 14-commodity series,[1] certain relationships were found whose analysis in mathematical form reveals the adequacy of the theory of constancy of spread per retail sale as an explanation of these contrasts.

INFLUENCE OF USUAL UNITS OF QUANTITY

When the percentage margins were plotted in a scatter diagram against the respective total 1923 retail values of the 14-commodities, there was found an inverse curvilinear relationship between the two magnitudes. The commodities with the greater total retail values had generally lower margins than those with the lesser total retail values. The proportion absorbed by distribution expense varied somewhat inversely with the respective total commodity values, as is shown statistically in Table 24 and visually by the bars in Figure 12. These bars are a graphic presentation of the fact that when the series of articles is arrayed in ascending order according to their total 1923 retail values, the corresponding percentage margins lie generally in descending order.

To illustrate the relationship, let three of the fourteen articles with widely differing values be considered,—northern

[1] See chap. iv, p. 75.

TABLE 24

RELATION BETWEEN MARGINS AND TOTAL ANNUAL RETAIL VALUES, NEW YORK METROPOLITAN AREA, FEBRUARY, 1923–MAY, 1924

Commodity	Total 1923 retail value	Percentage margin
	Dollars	Per cent
Northern potatoes	23,111,000	37
California oranges	22,419,000	41
Boxed apples	21,040,000	46
Barreled apples	17,936,000	49
Southern potatoes	15,855,000	38
Peaches	9,288,000	45
Yellow onions	9,037,000	53
Eastern lettuce	8,944,000	51
Cantaloupes	7,469,000	46
Sweet potatoes	4,601,000	44
Western lettuce	4,404,000	52
Southern cabbage	4,211,000	48
Northern cabbage	2,373,000	58
White onions	1,290,000	63

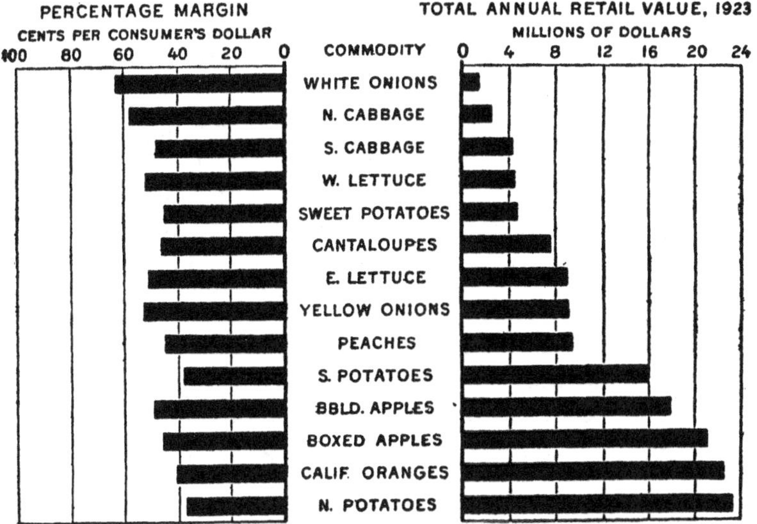

FIGURE 12

cabbage, barreled apples, California oranges. The items in the total retail value series are in descending order, thus:

Commodity	Total 1923 retail value	Margin
Northern cabbage....................	2.37 million dollars	58 per cent
Barreled apples.....................	17.94 " "	49 " "
California oranges..................	22.42 " "	41 " "

From observation of these arrays, the question may arise: Do not the differences in total retail value explain adequately the differences in percentage margins? Is not the lower margin on barreled apples, in comparison with that of northern cabbage, due simply to the fact that the metropolitan area as a whole spends more money per year for apples than it does for cabbage? Such a supposition might arise from the view that merchants could handle the articles which yield their principal income at less expense per dollar's worth of goods than commodities which bring them a minor return. The following mathematical analysis will serve to explain the meaning of the inverse association between total values and percentage margins.

Let the total annual retail value of any commodity be indicated by R, and its total annual wholesale value be represented by W. The difference between R and W will then represent the total annual expense of distributing the given article in the metropolitan area. The ratio of this total distribution expense to the total retail value, $\frac{R-W}{R}$, will then indicate the percentage margin for the given commodity.

The statement that margins vary inversely with total retail values is expressed in mathematical terms by the formula: $\frac{R-W}{R}$ varies as $\frac{1}{R}$. Now in the series of commodities, the percentage margin $\frac{R-W}{R}$ may be diminished concurrently with an increase in the total retail value R, by any one of three conditions affecting the relation between R and W, namely: (a) if R-W remains constant, (b) if R-W declines, (c) if R-W advances less rapidly than R increases. The last one of these conditions really embraces all three; for with constancy in R-W, or with a decline in R-W, the total retail value R would show greater increase than that of total distribution expense, R-W. The statement that the percentage margin varies inversely with the total retail value of an article therefore means merely that *within the commodity series an increase in total retail value is accompanied by a proportionally smaller increase in total distribution expense.* A satisfactory explanation of this peculiar relationship is needed to interpret the general inverse association between margins and total retail values.

In the three illustrative commodities, the total retail value, the total distribution expense, and the percentage margin for each, are:

Commodity	R Total retail value	R-W Total distribution expense	$\frac{R-W}{R}$ Margin
Northern cabbage ..	2.37 million dollars	1.38 million dollars	58 per cent
Barreled apples	17.94 " "	8.71 " "	49 " "
California oranges ..	22.42 " "	9.15 " "	41 " "

In each case a change in R is accompanied by a relatively smaller change in R-W:

Thus, while	R	for apples is	7.5 times	R	for cabbage,
yet	R-W	" " " only	6.3 "	R-W	" "
and	R	for oranges is	1.3 times	R	for apples,
but	R-W	" " " only	1.1 "	R-W	" "

Now the percentage margin for each commodity is a quotient derived by dividing the figure in the second column by that in the first column. The decline in the margin for apples (49) from that for cabbage (58), results from the fact that R-W for apples is only 6.3 times R-W for cabbage, while R for apples is 7.5 times R for cabbage. The margin for apples is therefore $\frac{6.3}{7.5} \times 58$, which is 49 per cent. Similarly, the decline in the percentage margin for oranges (41) from that for apples (49), results from the fact that R-W for oranges is only 1.1 times R-W for apples, whereas R for oranges is 1.3 times R for apples. The margin for oranges is therefore $\frac{1.1}{1.3} \times 49$, which is 41 per cent. Throughout the fourteen-commodity series, it may be demonstrated similarly that the inverse association between percentage margins and total retail value results from the fact that total retail value increases from one article to another more rapidly than does the total distribution expense.

It still remains to explain *why* increases in total retail values are accompanied by relatively smaller increases in distribution expense. The total retail value of any commodity may be conceived of as the product of (1) retail price per pound and (2) total number of pounds sold annually. The total distribution expense may be regarded either (a) as the product of price spread per pound and the total number of pounds, or (b) as the difference between total wholesale value and total retail value. If for any commodity, r represents the retail price per pound, w the wholesale price per pound, and P the total number of pounds sold in the metropolitan area in 1923, then the total retail value R is equivalent to r times P; the total wholesale value is equivalent to w times P; and the total distribution expense R-W is rP minus wP. The percentage margin is therefore $\frac{rP-wP}{rP}$. By cancelling out the P's in this fraction, the percentage margin becomes $\frac{r-w}{r}$. This means that for any commodity in the series the percentage margin is the same whether based on total values or on values per pound. The conclusion is, therefore, that percentage margins are independent of physical volume as a separate factor. Any influence exerted by physical volume is expressed already in the prices themselves.

The analysis shows that a difference in physical volumes of any two commodities affects R-W and R identically. The reason why R-W fails to increase as rapidly as R, within the series of articles, is that r-w does not increase as rapidly as r. In other words, the *price spread per pound does not increase proportionally with retail price per pound.*

Calculations from the per-pound figures[1] for the three illustrative commodities shows that an increase in retail price is accompanied by a relatively smaller gain in price spread:

Commodity	r Mean retail price per pound	w Mean wholesale price per pound[2]	r-w Mean price spread per pound	$\frac{r-w}{r}$ Margin
Northern cabbage....	5.20 cents	2.18 cents	3.02 cents	58 per cent
Barreled apples......	7.97 "	4.10 "	3.87 "	49 " "
California oranges ...	10.95 "	6.48 "	4.47 "	41 " "

The percentage margin for cabbage is the quotient of 3.02 divided by 5.20. The decline in the margin for apples to 49 per cent from 58, the margin for cabbage, results from the fact that while r-w for apples is only 1.28 times r-w for cabbage, yet r for apples is 1.53 times r for cabbage. The percentage margin for apples is therefore $\frac{1.28}{1.53}$ times 58, which is 49. Similarly for oranges, r-w is only 1.16 times r-w for apples, while r for oranges is 1.37 times

[1] See Appendix, page 140 for per pound figures of whole series.

[2] Adjusted for shrinkage in retailing.

r for apples. Hence the margin for oranges shows a decline from the margin for apples, because of the difference in these two ratios. It is $\frac{1.16}{1.37}$ times 49, which is 41 per cent.

In this indirect way is demonstrated the simple but significant fact that margin variations in the series of commodities are synonymous with varying relationships between distribution expense per pound and their respective retail prices per pound. The statement that one article has a lower percentage margin than another article is synonymous with the statement that the ratio of price spreads per pound is less than the ratio of the respective retail prices per pound. The margin for a given commodity is the same irrespective of the physical quantity of goods considered in computing it.

INFLUENCE OF THE NEW UNIT OF DISTRIBUTION

In the comparisons and analyses of different commodities thus far, the consumer's dollar's worth and the pound were the assumed common units of measurement. The differences noted in the expense of distribution per dollar's worth and per pound were treated as though they required explanation, but no satisfactory explanation of these differences was found.

Upon reflection, it is evident that no sound reason exists for either the margin per dollar's worth, or the price spread per pound, to be uniform for different articles. The principal expense incurred in distributing commodities arises from various services rendered by the distribution agencies. Now if more service is required to retail a dollar's worth or a pound of one article than to sell a dollar's worth or a pound of another article, the cost of the additional service is logically reflected in a higher retail price.

The amount of service given by the dealer with each dollar's worth of a commodity depends to a great extent upon the number of separate sales he must make to receive a dollar from his customers. This depends in turn upon the average size of sale to the individual consumer. While retail sales of some articles are prevailingly made in larger quantities and larger monetary amounts than are sales of other commodities, yet each sale irrespective of size or value entails an approximately uniform expense for retailer's service. Apportionment of the service expense on the basis of the dollar's worth or the pound ignores the contrast of different commodities in their service requirements. A logical means of comparison should place all commodities on a comparable service basis. This is done when comparisons are made on the basis of the individual retail sale.

HOW RETAIL PRICES ARE SET

The vital part of this theoretical analysis is the determination of how retail prices are set. Here the size of the sale to the consumer plays a dominant part.

It was shown that in the series of commodities the size of the retail sale varies inversely with the retail price per pound (as illustrated by the bars in Figure 4 on page 80). The commodities with low retail price per pound are sold to consumers in lots of several pounds at a time, whereas articles with high price per pound are sold in smaller lots. The average retail price of northern potatoes was about 4 cents a pound, and the prevailing size of sale was 6½ pounds. Western lettuce, whose retail price averaged about 15 cents per pound, had a prevailing size of sale of but 1½ pounds. For each of the three illustrative commodities, the retail price per pound and the number of pounds per retail sale were:

Commodity	Mean retail price per pound	Size of mean retail sale
Northern cabbage	5.20 cents	4.00 pounds
Barreled apples	7.97 "	3.00 "
California oranges	10.95 "	2.50 "

When these commodities are arranged in ascending order of retail price per pound, the size of retail sale is observed to be in descending order. This is representative of the general tendency for all commodities, as shown in Figure 4.

A means now appears for explaining what determines retail price per pound, and the price spread per pound. The difficulties arising from the unsuitableness of the pound as a unit for comparison of distribution factors are removed by using the standard retail sale as the unit of distribution. With the size-of-sale data, price spread may be computed per retail sale. The spread per sale is the product of the price spread per pound and the number of pounds per sale. For the three illustrative articles, the mean spread per pound, the mean size of the retail sale, and the mean spread per sale, are:

Commodity	Mean spread per pound	Mean size of Retail sale	Mean spread per retail sale
Northern cabbage	3.02 cents	4.00 pounds	12.1 cents
Barreled apples	3.87 "	3.00 "	11.6 "
California oranges....	4.47 "	2.50 "	11.2 "

When the commodities are arranged as above in ascending order of magnitude of spread per pound, the size of sale series is in descending order, as was shown to be true in the preceding instance with the price-per-pound series. The product of these two, shown as the mean spread per retail sale, is nearly constant, in consequence of the inverse relationship of the spread-per-pound series and the size-of-sale series. This is illustrative of the general tendency for all fourteen commodities, as was shown in Figure 5 on page 82.

The general conclusion is therefore reached that *retail prices are set at such levels above wholesale prices as will tend to make the spread between wholesale and retail values of the standard retail sale the same for all commodities.*

This theory of a constant spread per sale for all commodities throws light upon several problems of distribution. It provides the key needed to explain why the portion of the consumer's dollar which is absorbed in the expense of city distribution should be greater for some articles than it is for others. It indicates the existence of a distinctive price-setting practice, based upon the prevailing size of the consumer's individual purchase. Furthermore, it shows that any significant relationship between physical volumes and margins may be traced to associated differences in size of sale.

SUMMARY OF APPLICATION OF SIZE-OF-SALE THEORY

The differences in percentage margins within the commodity series, ranging from 37 for northern potatoes to 63 for white onions, come about from use of the dollar's worth of goods as the unit of measurement. These differences are merely a reflection of the fact that it costs more to distribute a dollar's worth of some commodities than a dollar's worth of others. The assumption that the distribution expense per dollar's worth should be the same for all commodities is illogical. Analysis shows that more actual service on the part of dealers is required in distributing a dollar's worth of some articles than in the case of others, because of differences in their prevailing sizes of sale. The difference in retailer's practice arises from the buying habits of consumers, which are variable with different commodities.

Differences in percentage margins of different commodities thus result from using the dollar's worth, with its varying service requirements, as the distribution unit. When the individual retail sale is taken as a new unit of distribution, the actual margin per sale is nearly constant for all the commodities, and no appreciable differences remain to be explained.

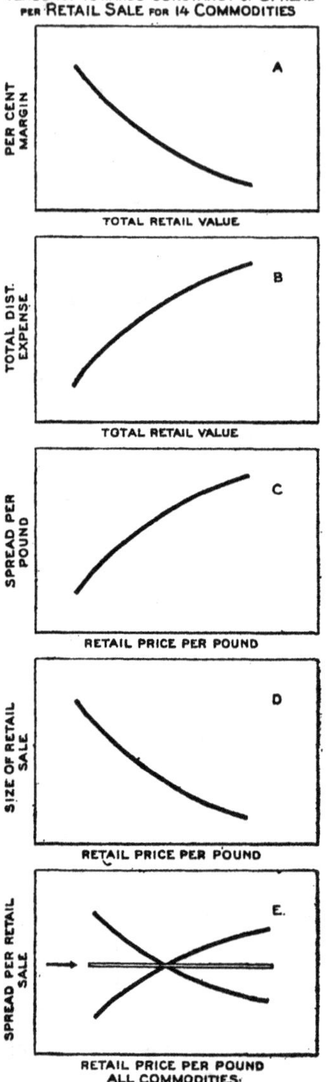

a. Among the fourteen commodities there is an inverse curvilinear relationship between percentage margins and total retail values.

b. The above association is the result of a direct curvilinear relationship between total distribution expense and total retail value, with the curve bending toward the total-retail-value axis.

c. Analysis of the relationship between total distribution expense and total retail value reveals a direct curvilinear association between spread per pound and retail price per pound, with the curve bending toward the retail price axis.

d. There is an inverse curvilinear relationship between size of the retail sale and retail price per pound.

e. Spread per retail sale is the product of spread per pound and number of pounds per retail sale. Combination of the direct relationship in c and the inverse relationship in d results in a tendency towards constant spread per retail sale for all commodities.

FIGURE 13

The logical steps in application of the principle of variability in size of the retail sale as an explanation of differences in percentage margins are shown by means of the five illustrative diagrams in Figure 13.

LIMITATIONS OF PERCENTAGE DIFFERENTIALS IN PRICE COMPARISONS

Comparison of percentages of different basic magnitudes are found to incur certain mathematical difficulties, which may vitiate the meaning of such comparisons when used to analyze price situations. This made it necessary to abandon the original plan of making detailed comparisons of margins as percentages of retail prices, and instead of these to compare actual prices or price spreads.

The percentage-margin concept assumes a constant money expenditure by the consumer, representing a dollar's worth of goods under given price conditions. Any variation in retail price entails, therefore, a change in the quantity of goods obtained for one dollar. Hence the margin represents, in cents of the consumer's dollar, the spread between buying-price and selling-price for a variable quantity of goods, whose volume changes with any change in the selling price. Use of differentials between percentage margins, to measure the relative efficiency of a given money outlay under varying price conditions, is therefore logically unsound.

The difficulty in evaluating percentage differentials may be illustrated by attempting a comparison of percentage margins in two types of retail stores. The general margin in independent credit-delivery stores for the whole commodity series was found to be 47 per cent of the mean retail price. In cash-carry stores it was only 42 per cent of the retail price. This is equivalent to saying that of a dollar's outlay by the consumer, 47 cents is required in a credit-delivery store to cover distribution expense, which leaves 53 cents to purchase goods in the wholesale market; out of the dollar similarly spent in a cash-carry store, only 42 cents is required for distribution expense, and 58 cents remain to purchase goods in the wholesale market.

The differential of 5 cents in the consumer's dollar outlay in the two store-types, thus proves to be quite otherwise than the apparent difference of 5 per cent of the retail price. Of the dollar expenditure under the two conditions, 58 cents of the cash-carry customer's money is invested in goods in the wholesale market, whereas only 53 cents of the credit-delivery customer's money is so used. Hence for his dollar outlay the cash-carry customer obtains $\frac{58}{53}$ times the quantity of goods obtained by the credit-delivery customer. For an identical quantity of goods, therefore, the cash-carry customer would pay only $\frac{53}{58}$ of the other's outlay. This fraction, for the cash-carry store, is 91.4 per cent of the amount required for the same quantity of goods in the credit-delivery store. The actual differential between retail prices in the two store-types is therefore 100 minus 91.4, or 8.6 per cent of the credit-delivery price, instead of the assumed 5 per cent.

If it were desired to indicate the differential in terms of the cash-carry store, then the corresponding inverted fraction, $\frac{58}{53}$, should be used to indicate the credit-delivery price. This is 109.4 per cent of the cash-carry price. The selling price for a given quantity of goods in a credit-delivery store is thus 9.4 per cent higher than the price for the same quantity in a cash-carry store.

The difficulty just illustrated exists wherever comparisons are attempted of percentages derived from varying or non-comparable bases. Any attempt to make measurable comparisons of prices by comparing their percentage margins is therefore likely to confuse and to distort the actual differences.

CHAPTER VII

General Conclusions

The statistical analyses embodied in this study have revealed three features in the metropolitan distribution system of outstanding significance as determinants of the outlay required from city consumers for their perishable food supply.

The first of these is the remarkable influence of the purchasing habits of consumers on the expense of city distribution. The prevailing size of the individual retail sale is demonstrated to determine in large measure the proportion of the consumer's expenditure which is absorbed in the distribution process. The price spread necessary to cover the services required in bringing supplies from the city wholesale market to metropolitan consumers is found to be fairly constant per individual retail sale for different commodities, irrespective of the physical size of sale.

Selling prices seem to be fixed by the retailer at a point sufficiently above cost to cover the expense of service which he renders and to yield a fairly uniform money spread per sale. The extent of service involved in distributing a given quantity of goods thus fixes the proportion which the retailer must add to cover his operating expenses. The larger the consumer's purchase, the smaller is the proportion of his expenditure which is absorbed by distribution charges, and the greater is the proportion left to pay for merchandise.

All distribution services have to be paid for out of the price received by the retailer for the individual sale. Since every sale is a profit-making opportunity, the retailer must so apportion his expense among his individual sales as to yield a living outside of the cost of the goods he sells and the distribution expense which he undergoes. The great number of conveniences given to consumers under present methods of city distribution must be paid for by the spread between the original cost of the goods and their selling price. Maintenance of a continuous, well-selected stock, readily accessible in wide variety at all times, and the breaking up of this stock into small portions to meet the day-to-day needs of consumers in the immediate neighborhood, require a large outlay by the retailer for the service involved. The expense occasioned in rendering these services is conditioned more by the number of separate transactions required to dispose of his goods, than by the gross volume of goods sold. The price to consumers is therefore established at a point that will assure a fairly uniform money spread on each individual transaction. The retailer has to adjust his price policy to the prevailing buying habits of his customers. Retail prices are therefore scaled to accord with consumers' predominant practice of small, oft-repeated purchases.

A second significant factor in the expense of distributing fruits and vegetables is shown to be the form of organization or management of the retail store. The standardized operation of chain stores, with centralized purchase of supplies in large quantities, gives this form of operation distinct advantages. Although the chain-store system has not been applied extensively to specialized retailing of fruits and vegetables, this field appears to offer an opportunity for promoting economies in distribution.

Offsetting the economy of the chain form of operation, distinct advantages are offered by the independently operated neighborhood store. Its personal atmosphere, its readiness to serve the preferences of individual customers, the generally greater variety and wider choice of qualities, give the independent store a strong hold upon its local clientele. The preference between chain store and unit store is a matter of the relative emphasis upon economy and convenience. One portion of the consuming public prefers the fuller advantages of the neighborhood store with its higher prices, while another portion prefers to forego these advantages for the economy of the lower prices of chain stores.

This study shows further that the special services involved in delivery of goods and extension of credit require a substantial addition to the consumers' food outlay. Stores which operate on a cash-and-carry basis are able to sell goods at prices materially lower than those which have a credit-and-delivery policy. While many consumers doubtless find the convenience of the credit-and-delivery store well worth the added expense, those to whom economy is the first consideration may enjoy a considerable saving by buying from stores whose prices are based upon a cash-and-carry policy.

From the foregoing analyses it appears that material economies of distribution are possible through closer coordination of the functions of distributing agencies. In the chain-store plan of operation, an important factor in cutting down distribution expense appears to be the centralization of purchases whereby supplies are bought by the distributor in large quantities, thus economizing in the outlay for intermediate handling. Independent retailers might embody much of this buying efficiency of chain-store organizations by an organized plan of centralized purchasing, which would enable them still to retain the personal advantages of the independent neighborhood unit store. Proprietors of unit stores in a given locality could unite for the purchase of supplies through a common agent or through one of their number delegated to perform this function for the group. Such combination of requirements into large orders would not only enable them to purchase supplies at more favorable prices, but would also eliminate much of the expense arising from duplication in handling and inward delivery. It would further save much time that is otherwise spent by individual retailers in repeated trips to jobbing markets.

To what extent is it feasible to stimulate the practice of larger-sized purchases by consumers, for the purpose of reducing the expense of city distribution? It may be argued that consumers find it impracticable to buy perishable commodities otherwise than in oft-repeated small amounts for their day-to-day needs. Semi-staple articles, however, such as potatoes, onions, apples, and oranges, can ordinarily be stored in family quarters for several days or a week without serious loss. With these articles several days' supply could be combined in a single purchase of considerable size. While it is argued that the limitation of storage facilities in many city homes prevents buying in large quantities, it cannot be doubted that a great deal of the small-quantity buying by consumers is unwarranted by conditions and is simply the result of habit and lack of foresight.

A means for stimulating larger-size purchases by consumers might be provided through adoption by retailers of a plan for advertising and selling goods under a standard "cost-plus-service" policy. The selling price of commodities might be stated as consisting of two independent portions, one of which is required to cover the actual cost of goods to the retailer, while the other covers the expense of making the individual sale. The amount of the first portion would vary according to the quantity of goods sold to the customer, based upon a uniform price per unit, such as a pound, quart, head, or dozen of commodity. The second portion would be a constant fixed amount, regardless of the quantity of goods sold per transaction. Hence the larger the quantity purchased by an individual consumer, the smaller would be the proportion of the outlay required for distribution service. In a similar way there might be a special addition to the fixed sale charge, for credit and delivery. Such a policy, carefully and impartially carried out, would emphasize to consumers the economy of larger-size purchases, and would be an inducement to them to increase the size of the retailer's sale.

The logical consequence of larger-size sales would be less frequent sales to individual customers. This would reduce the number of retail transactions needed to distribute a given quantity of goods to a community. From the resulting reduction in requirements for distribution service, retailers would find need for less extensive personnel. A large store might perhaps dispense with one of its employees. A small store, whose business was not sufficient to fully occupy the time of two persons, might accommodate the former volume of business with one person, or it might expand its trade to occupy fully the former staff, thus increasing the total volume of goods sold in the same number of individual transactions. Either cutting down the personnel to handle a fixed quantity of goods, or employing the same personnel to handle greater volume, means a reduction in proportional outlay for wages and salaries. Since this outlay is the principal item of expense in retailing, here is the most effective place to reduce the retailer's mark-up on the cost of his goods. A general increase in the size of the individual sale would thus make possible a reduction in the price-spread, and a lowering of prices to consumers.

It might be argued, on the other hand, that with less frequent sales to consumers the retailers would have fewer opportunities for profit, for every sale is a profit-making opportunity. One might say, therefore, that the retailer would have to increase his portion on each sale in order to attain his previous income. From this would result the same scale of prices on the enlarged unit sales as on the previous small unit sales. This reasoning disregards the fact, however, that with larger-size sales it would be possible by expanding the reach of his trade to reduce distribution expense for service per physical unit of commodity, thus restoring the former number of transactions which the retailer is equipped to handle. The lowering of prices from the competition of enterprising rivals would tend to reduce his former profit, unless it were offset by an increased volume of trade.

It is generally conceded that in recent years the number of retailers has increased very materially in proportion to the growth in population. It is so easy for people with limited capital and experience to engage in small-scale retailing that men are tempted to overcrowd the field. While one cannot state dogmatically the exact number of retailers that are needed to supply the needs of a community adequately and economically, there appear to be far more retail stores in some parts of the metropolitan area than are necessary to supply adequately the requirements of the population. From limited studies of costs of operation in stores of different sizes,[1] it is apparent that stores which have a very small volume of trade do not operate as economically as do the large-sized units, because a disproportionate amount of the retailer's income is required to meet overhead costs.

The logical outcome of larger-size sales would thus appear to be the elimination of small uneconomical stores which are distributing least efficiently, and to concentrate the trade of a community in a reduced number of stores, each handling a larger volume of goods. Such a reduction in numbers could diminish the tax on the community arising from what the superfluous stores pay in the form of rent, both by cut-

[1] See chapter ii, pp. 48-9.

ting down the number of rent-paying stores and by reducing the competition for store space, thereby lowering the rent scale. Thus could be diminished the second-largest item in the retailer's expense of doing business. The two principal taxes on a community in supplying its food requirements—wages and rent—could thus be reduced by the general adoption of larger-size purchases by consumers.

Since the practice of retailers is determined largely by the demands of consumers, improvement in the efficiency of distribution by means of larger-size transactions depends upon participation by the general body of consumers. The successful adoption of measures that would lead to more economical distribution rests largely therefore with individual consumers. It behooves persons who make the family purchases of perishables to become familiar with the conditions of metropolitan marketing, so that they may appreciate the factors involved in city distribution and the conditions which determine real values in their own purchases. There are simple and obvious ways whereby individual consumers may foster conditions to reduce the expense of city distribution. By planning the family food requirements well in advance, the day-to-day needs of a household may be anticipated and thus combined in a minimum number of separate purchases. Grouping a customer's orders for various articles enables the retailer to economize his time by filling them together instead of performing a number of separate operations. Such concentration of orders is of particular significance where goods are to be delivered. The avoidance of rush orders and last-moment demands enables the retailer to distribute the use of his time throughout the day, and thus to economize in expense for personnel. Confining family trading to a regular retailer enables him to estimate more accurately the requirements of his trade, so that his purchases of goods may be made with less risk of loss from unsold portions. Besides such general suggestions, this study has revealed that the expense of retailing may be reduced materially by cash payment for goods when they are purchased by the consumer and by elimination of deliveries.

A determining factor in city distribution expense has been shown to be the size and value of the standard retail sale. The portion of the consumer's outlay taken by the retailer is fixed largely by this factor, and its variations thus explain the variations in city margins among different commodities. Besides this factor, the form of store management and the policy in regard to credit and delivery service have a very material influence in determining the portion of the consumer's outlay which is absorbed in city distribution.

It thus appears that of the contribution which the consumer makes for *convenience,* one of the most expensive conveniences is the *additional service* that is required from the retailer by the oft-repeated individual sales of small quantities of goods. Increasing the average size of consumers' purchases would thus tend to lower the cost of perishables to the metropolitan population. This would enable consumers to purchase an increased proportion of perishables with their present monetary outlay. By increasing the proportion of fruits and vegetables in the total food consumption, it would promote the general health, without increasing the cost of living. Neither would there be a reduction in the prices paid to producers of the goods. In fact the increased demand attendant upon lower prices to consumers would provide them a larger market. Increasing the prevailing size of the individual sale would thus be of benefit to two large portions of the nation's population. This benefit would be obtained by the simple process of narrowing the gap between what the producer receives and what the consumer pays, without changing the methods or agencies of distribution.

The present study is offered not as a complete analysis of distribution expense, but rather as a charting of certain significant factors and of their relative significance. An attempt has been made to *identify the conditions* that account for price differences, and to *determine the extent* of these differences under varying market conditions. Only one phase of the broad distribution question, that dealing with price differences, has been considered here. No attempt has been made to measure quantities or to account for differences in consumer demand under varying conditions. Such a study would require the recording of actual quantities sold per sale in a large number of individual transactions, and the relative frequency of individual sales. Such an analysis would show the effects of variations in individual sales, as this study has shown them in the mass. It is desirable to determine the relative strength of forces that account for the price-differences here presented. This study provides a basis and a starting-point for such analyses.

With all the refinements of organization that may be made in city distribution, the task of providing food to metropolitan populations will continue to involve breaking up the large centralized stocks of goods that arrive each year in the wholesale market, into millions of separate small parcels for individual daily consumption. The effectiveness of any program that undertakes to reduce general distribution expense thus depends fundamentally upon the basic proposition of reducing this expense for the individual retail sale. Demonstration of the large part played by the size of sale in fixing this expense, and establishment of the standard retail sale as a distinct unit for measuring it, are therefore contributions of primary importance.

The application of the present study is not limited to the

marketing of perishable commodities. The principles here set forth have much wider significance, for they apply to the distribution of all consumers' goods that are sold in variable small quantities. These results are significant throughout the general field of retail distribution.

STATISTICAL APPENDIX

TERMINOLOGY

Spread—Difference between wholesale and retail
(a) prices per pound,
(b) values per sale,
(c) values per car.

Margin—Spread expressed as percentage of retail price.

Mark-up—Spread expressed as percentage of wholesale price or of jobbing price.

Value—Product of price per pound and number of pounds per unit considered (i. e. per sale, per car, or for total commodity).

Total Distribution Expense—Difference between total wholesale value and total retail value in 1923.

SYMBOLS USED IN APPENDIX TABLES[1]

A Number of price quotations
C Spread per car
D Spread per standard retail sale
E Number of cars received in New York City, 1923
H Differential in spread per car
I Index of variability of price
J Mean jobber's price per unit
K Differential in value of standard retail sale
L Number of pounds per unit at wholesale
M Per cent margin
N Number of units per car
P Mean price per pound
Q Mean number of pounds per sale
R Mean retail price per unit
S Mean number of sales per car
U Basic physical unit
V Mean value per car
W Mean wholesale price per unit
X Per cent of wholesale unit sold at retail, allowing for shrinkage
Z Mean value of standard sale

SUBSCRIPTS

a All stores
c Chain stores
f Fruit and vegetable (unit) stores
g Grocery (unit) stores
j Jobber
r Retail
u Unit stores
w Wholesale
(1) Credit-delivery
(2) Cash-delivery
(3) Cash-carry

The subscripts serve as modifiers of the large symbols; for example, "Pra" represents "Mean retail price per pound in all stores", and "Kulu2" represents "Differential in value of standard retail sale (adjusted) between credit-delivery unit stores and cash-delivery unit stores," etc.

[1] By means of the symbols and formulae in column captions, the derivation of any series may be traced to the original data. Thus, Column 22 is "Pra" or the "Mean Retail Price per Pound in All Stores". If it is desired to know how this series was derived from the original data, by referring to its formula "Ra/LX" it is found to be the quotient of the mean retail price per unit in all stores and the number of pounds sold at retail from the wholesale unit.

ANALYSIS OF COMMODITY (ALL STORE TYPES)

	Conversion Units					
	Basic Physical Unit	Number of Units Per Car	Number of Pounds Per Unit at Wholesale	Number of Wholesale Unit Sold at Retail, Allowing for Shrinkage	Pounds Sold at Retail from Wholesale Unit	Number of Pounds Per Car
Column No.	1	2	3	4	5	6
Formula	..	..	..	..	LX	NL
Symbol	U	N	L	X	..	..
Commodity:	Package	Number	Pounds	Per cent	Pounds	Pounds
Northern potatoes	cwt.	400	100	95	95	40,000
Southern potatoes	cwt.	330	100	92	92	33,000
California oranges	std. box	415	75	100	75	32,000
Peaches	24qt. crt.	500	35	95	33	17,500
Sweet potatoes	cwt.	225	100	90	90	22,500
Cantaloupes	std. crt.	340	60	100	60	20,400
Boxed apples	std. box	750	40	100	40	30,000
Southern cabbage	cwt.	210	100	90	90	21,000
Barreled apples	barrel	175	150	90	135	26,000
Eastern lettuce	3doz. hpr.	400	34	100	34	13,600
Western lettuce	4doz. crt.	320	48	100	48	15,400
Yellow onions	cwt.	250	100	95	95	25,000
Northern cabbage	cwt.	300	100	90	90	30,000
White onions	cwt.	250	100	100	95	25,000
Weighted mean	....	......	......	95.1	......	28,100

ANALYSIS OF COMMODITY (ALL STORE TYPES)—*Continued*

	Total Volume Received 1923				Total Volume Sold at Retail 1923	
	Number of Cars Received New York, 1923	Percentage of Total Cars Received 1923—14 commodities	Total Pounds Received New York, 1923	Percentage of Total Pounds Received 1923—14 commodities	Total Pounds Sold at Retail, 1923	Percentage of Total Pounds Sold at Retail 1923—14 commodities
Column No.	7	8	9	9a	10	10a
Formula	..	..	ENL	..	ENLX	..
Symbol	E	..	..	..	..	..
Commodity:	Cars	Per cent	Thousands of pounds	Per cent	Thousands of pounds	Percent
Northern potatoes	14,910	20.2	596,400	28.8	566,600	28.8
Southern potatoes	7,109	9.7	234,600	11.3	215,800	11.0
California oranges	6,584	8.9	210,700	10.2	210,700	10.7
Peaches	4,679	6.4	81,900	4.0	77,800	4.0
Sweet potatoes	2,556	3.5	57,500	2.8	51,750	2.6
Cantaloupes	4,803	6.5	98,000	4.7	98,000	5.0
Boxed apples	6,444	8.7	193,300	9.3	193,300	9.8
Southern cabbage	2,379	3.2	50,000	2.4	45,000	2.3
Barreled apples	9,515	12.9	247,400	12.0	222,700	11.3
Eastern lettuce	5,053	6.9	68,700	3.3	68,700	3.5
Western lettuce	1,953	2.7	30,100	1.5	30,100	1.5
Yellow onions	5,395	7.3	134,900	6.5	128,200	6.5
Northern cabbage	1,689	2.3	50,700	2.5	45,600	2.3
White onions	600	.8	15,000	.7	14,250	.7
Total	73,669	100	2,069,200	100	1,968,500	100

ANALYSIS OF COMMODITY (ALL STORE TYPES)—*Continued*

	Price Per Unit					
	Mean Retail Price Per Unit, All Stores	Mean Retail Price Per Unit, Unit Stores	Mean Wholesale Price Per Unit (All Stores)	Mean Wholesale Price Per Unit (Unit Stores)	Mean Jobbers' Price Per Unit (Unit Stores)	Index of Wholesale Price Variability (Mean weekly change expressed as percentage of season's mean price)
Column No.	11	12	13	14	15	16
Formula	..	..	..	..	..	..
Symbol	Ra	Ru	Wa	Wu	Ju	Iw
Commodity:	Dollars	Dollars	Dollars	Dollars	Dollars	Per cent
Northern potatoes	3.87	4.01	2.43	2.48	2.73	3.2
Southern potatoes	6.76[1]	..	4.18[1]	..	4.72[1]	11.8
California oranges	8.21	8.37	4.86	4.84	5.42	9.2
Peaches	3.97	3.97	2.20	2.18	2.56	24.1
Sweet potatoes	8.00	8.44	4.44	4.54	5.14	5.4
Cantaloupes	4.57	4.55	2.45	2.40	2.80	22.8
Boxed apples	4.35	4.47	2.33	2.37	2.88	4.6
Southern cabbage	8.42	8.63	4.42	4.52	5.43	25.9
Barreled apples	10.76	11.06	5.53	5.56	6.41	8.0
Eastern lettuce	4.43	4.55	2.16	2.20	2.78	26.4
Western lettuce	7.05	7.14	3.37	3.36	3.90	19.6
Yellow onions	6.70	6.80	3.17	3.17	3.67	13.5
Northern cabbage	4.68	4.85	1.96	2.02	2.49	12.8
White onions	8.59	8.88	3.22	3.24	4.28	..

[1] Based on 12 months' average prices.

Analysis of Commodity (All Store Types)—*Continued*

	Value Per Car					Price Per Pound		
	Retail Value Per Car (All Stores)	Wholesale Value Per Car (All Stores)	Retail Value Per Car (Unit Stores)	Wholesale Value Per Car (Unit Stores)	Jobbing Value Per Car (Unit Stores)	Mean Retail Price Per Pound (All Stores)	Mean Wholesale Price Per Pound (All Stores)	Mean Jobbing Price Per Pound (Unit Stores)
Column No.	17	18	19	20	21	22	23	24
Formula	NRa	NWa	NRu	NWu	NJu	$\frac{Ra}{LX}$	$\frac{Wa}{L}$	$\frac{Ju}{L}$
Symbol	Vra	VWa	Vru	Vwu	Vju	Pra	Pwa	Pju
Commodity:	Dollars	Dollars	Dollars	Dollars	Dollars	Cents	Cents	Cents
Northern potatoes	1,550	970	1,605	990	1,090	4.1	2.4	2.7
Southern potatoes	2,230[1]	1,380[1]	2,230	1,380	1,560	7.4[1]	4.2[1]	4.7
California oranges	3,465	2,015	3,475	2,010	2,250	11.0	6.5	7.2
Peaches	1,985	1,100	1,985	1,090	1,280	11.9	6.3	7.3
Sweet potatoes	1,800	1,000	1,900	1,020	1,155	8.9	4.4	5.1
Cantaloupes	1,555	835	1,545	815	950	7.6	4.1	4.7
Boxed apples	3,265	1,750	3,355	1,780	2,160	10.9	5.8	7.2
Southern cabbage	1,770	930	1,815	950	1,140	9.4	4.4	5.4
Barreled apples	1,885	970	1,935	975	1,120	8.0	3.7	4.3
Eastern lettuce	1,770	865	1,820	880	1,110	13.0	6.4	8.2
Western lettuce	2,255	1,080	2,285	1,075	1,250	14.7	7.0	8.1
Yellow onions	1,675	745	1,700	795	920	7.1	3.2	3.7
Northern cabbage	1,405	590	1,455	605	745	5.2	2.0	2.5
White onions	2,150	805	2,220	810	1,070	9.0	3.2	4.3
Weighted mean	$2,065	$1,145	$2,105	$1,150	$1,330	7.7c.	4.1c	4.7c.

[1] Based on 12 months' average prices.

Analysis of Commodity (All Store Types)—*Continued*

	Total Value of Commodity 1923				
	Retail Value of Commodity, 1923, (All Stores)	Percentage of Total Retail Value (14 commodities)	Wholesale Value of Commodity 1923 (All Stores)	Percentage of Total Wholesale Value (14 commodities)	Jobbing Value of Commodity 1923 (assuming all cars were sold through jobbers)
Column No.	25	25a	26	26a	27
Formula	VraE	..	VwaE	..	VjuE
Symbol	..	..	..	..	..
Commodity:	Thousands of dollars	Per cent	Thousands of dollars	Per cent	Thousands of dollars
Northern potatoes	23,111	15.3	14,465	17.2	16,252
Southern potatoes	15,855[1]	10.4	9,810[1]	11.6	11,090
California oranges	22,419	14.8	13,265	15.7	14,814
Peaches	9,288	6.1	5,145	6.1	5,989
Sweet potatoes	4,601	3.0	2,555	3.0	2,952
Cantaloupes	7,469	4.9	4,011	4.8	4,563
Boxed apples	21,040	13.8	11,277	13.4	13,919
Southern cabbage	4,211	2.8	2,210	2.6	2,712
Barreled apples	17,936	11.8	9,230	11.0	10,657
Eastern lettuce	8,944	5.9	4,370	5.2	5,609
Western lettuce	4,404	2.9	2,110	2.5	2,441
Yellow onions	9,037	5.9	4,290	5.1	4,963
Northern cabbage	2,373	1.6	995	1.2	1,258
White onions	1,290	.8	485	.6	642
Total	151,978	100	84,218	100	97,861

[1] Based on 12 months' average prices.

ANALYSIS OF COMMODITY (ALL STORE TYPES)—*Continued*

	Size of Standard Sale			
	Range in Size of Retail Sale	Mean Number of Pounds Per Retail Sale	Range in Size of Jobbers' Sale	Mean Number of Pounds Per Jobbers' Sale
Column No.	27	28	29	30
Formula	..	..	..	..
Symbol	.	Qr	..	Qj
Commodity:	Pounds	Pounds	Pounds	Pounds
Northern potatoes	5 to 8	6.50	200–250	225
Southern potatoes	3 to 4.5	3.75	165–200	183
California oranges	2 to 3	2.50	75–93	84
Peaches	1.5 to 3	2.25	60–70	65
Sweet potatoes	2.5 to 3	2.75	50–100	75
Cantaloupes	3 to 3.5	3.25	90–102	96
Boxed apples	1.5 to 3	2.25	40–120	80
Southern cabbage	2 to 3.5	2.75	90–100	95
Barreled apples	2.5 to 3.5	3.00	50–150	100
Eastern lettuce	1.5 to 2	1.75	48–60	54
Western lettuce	1 to 2	1.50	48–68	58
Yellow onions	2.5 to 4	3.25	100–120	110
Northern cabbage	3 to 5	4.00	120–130	125
White onions	1.5 to 3	2.25	..	100
Weighted mean	..	3.28	..	112

ANALYSIS OF COMMODITY (ALL STORES AND UNIT STORES)

	Mean Value of Standard Sale				
	Mean Retail Price Per Pound (All Stores)	Mean Value of Standard Retail Sale (All Stores)	Mean Retail Price Per Pound (Unit Stores)	Mean Value of Standard Retail Sale (Unit Stores)	Mean Value of Standard Jobbers' Sale (Unit Stores)
Column No.	31	32	33	34	35
Formula	$\frac{RA}{LX}$	QrPra	$\frac{Ru}{LX}$	QrPru	QjPju
Symbol	Pra	Zra	Pru	Zru	Zju
Commodity:	Cents	Cents	Cents	Cents	Dollars
Northern potatoes	4.1	26.7	4.2	27.3	6.08
Southern potatoes	7.4[1]	27.8[1]	7.4	27.8	8.60
California oranges	11.0	27.5	11.2	28.0	6.05
Peaches	11.9	26.8	12.0	27.0	4.75
Sweet potatoes	8.9	24.5	9.4	25.9	3.83
Cantaloupes	7.6	24.7	7.6	24.7	4.51
Boxed apples	10.9	24.7	11.2	25.2	5.76
Southern cabbage	9.4	25.9	9.6	26.4	5.13
Barreled apples	8.0	24.0	8.2	24.6	4.30
Eastern lettuce	13.0	22.8	13.4	23.5	4.43
Western lettuce	14.7	22.1	14.9	22.4	4.70
Yellow onions	7.1	23.1	7.2	23.4	4.07
Northern cabbage	5.2	20.8	5.4	21.6	3.13
White onions	9.0	20.3	9.3	20.9	4.30
Weighted mean	7.7	25.3	7.9	25.9	5.25

[1] Based on 12 months' data, 1923.

ANALYSIS OF COMMODITY (ALL STORE TYPES)

	Number of Sales						
	Mean Number of Retail Sales Per Car	Mean Number of Jobbers' Sales Per Car.	Mean Number of Retail Sales Per Jobbers' Sale	Total Number Retail Sales Year 1923	Percent of Total Number Retail Sales—14 commodities	Total Number of Jobbers' Sales—Year 1923	Percent of Total Number Jobbers' Sales—14 commodities
Column No.	36	37	38	39	39a	40	40a
Formula	Vra / Zra	NL / Qj	Sr / Sj	ESr	..	ESj	..
Symbol	Sr	Sj	..	..	..	..	..
Commodity:	Sales	Sales	Sales	Thousands of Sales	Per cent	Thousands of Sales	Per cent
Northern potatoes	5,805	178	33	86,553	14.4	2,654	14.4
Southern potatoes	8,020	180	45	57,014	9.5	1,280	6.9
California oranges	12,380	381	32	81,510	13.6	2,509	13.6
Peaches	7,405	269	28	34,648	5.8	1,259	6.8
Sweet potatoes	7,345	300	24	18,774	3.1	767	4.2
Cantaloupes	6,295	213	30	30,235	5.0	1,023	5.5
Boxed apples	13,220	375	35	85,190	14.2	2,417	13.1
Southern cabbage	6,835	221	31	16,260	2.7	526	2.8
Barreled apples	7,855	260	30	73,739	12.3	2,474	13.4
Eastern lettuce	7,765	252	31	39,237	6.6	1,273	6.9
Western lettuce	10,205	266	38	19,930	3.3	519	2.8
Yellow onions	7,250	227	32	39,114	6.5	1,225	6.6
Northern cabbage	6,755	240	28	11,409	1.9	405	2.2
White onions	10,590	250	43	6,354	1.1	150	.8
Total	..	..	..	599,967	100	18,481	100
Weighted mean	8,145	250	32.5	..	..	..	..

Analysis of Commodity (All Stores and Unit Stores)

	Spread Per Standard Retail Sale			
	Total Spread (All Stores)	Total Spread (Unit Stores)	Retailer's Spread (Unit Stores)	Jobber's Spread (Unit Stores)
Column No.	41	42	43	44
Formula	MtaZra	MtuZru	MruZru	MjuZru
Symbol	Dta	Dtu	Dru	Dju
Commodity:	Cents	Cents	Cents	Cents
Northern potatoes	9.9	10.4	8.7	1.7
Southern potatoes	10.6[1]	10.8	9.2	1.6
California oranges ...	11.3	11.8	9.8	2.0
Peaches	12.1	12.2	9.7	2.5
Sweet potatoes	11.0	11.9	10.1	1.8
Cantaloupes	11.4	11.6	9.6	2.0
Boxed apples	11.4	11.8	9.1	2.7
Southern cabbage	12.4	12.7	9.8	2.9
Barreled apples	11.8	12.3	10.3	2.0
Eastern lettuce	11.5	12.2	9.2	3.0
Western lettuce	11.6	11.9	10.1	1.8
Yellow onions	12.2	12.4	10.8	1.6
Northern cabbage	12.1	12.5	10.6	1.9
White onions	12.8	13.4	10.9	2.5
Weighted mean	11.3	11.8	9.7	2.1

[1] Based on 12 months' data, 1923.

ANALYSIS OF COMMODITY (ALL STORES AND UNIT STORES)

	Spread Per Car				Total Distribution Expense of Commodity, 1923	
	Total Spread (All Stores)	Total Spread (Unit Stores)	Retailer's Spread (Unit Stores)	Jobber's Spread (Unit Stores)	(All Stores)	Percentage of Total for 14 commodities
Column No.	45	46	47	48	49	49a
Formula	Vra-Vwa	Vru-Vwu	Vru-Vju	Vju-Vwu	ECta	..
Symbol	Cta	Ctu	Cru	Cju	..	..
Commodity:	Dollars	Dollars	Dollars	Dollars	Thousands of dollars	Per cent
Northern potatoes	580	615	515	100	8,646	12.8
Southern potatoes	850[1]	850	670	180	6,045	8.9
California oranges	1,390	1,465	1,225	240	9,154	13.5
Peaches	885	895	705	190	4,143	6.1
Sweet potatoes	800	880	745	135	2,046	3.0
Cantaloupes	720	730	595	135	3,458	5.1
Boxed apples	1,515	1,575	1,195	380	9,763	14.4
Southern cabbage	840	865	675	190	2,001	2.9
Barreled apples	915	960	815	145	8,706	12.9
Eastern lettuce	905	940	710	230	4,574	6.8
Western lettuce	1,175	1,210	1,035	175	2,294	3.4
Yellow onions	880	905	780	125	4,747	7.0
Northern cabbage	815	850	710	140	1,378	2.0
White onions	1,345	1,410	1,159	260	805	1.2
Total	..	..	..	..	67,760	100
Weighted mean	920	955	775	180	..	..

[1] Based on 12 months' data, 1923.

ANALYSIS OF COMMODITY (ALL STORES AND UNIT STORES)

	Percentage Margin (Cents of Consumer's Dollar)				Percentage Mark-up from Wholesale	
	Total Margin (All Stores)	Total Margin (Unit Stores)	Retailer's Margin (Unit Stores)	Jobber's Margin (Unit Stores)	Total Mark-up (All Stores)	Jobber's Mark-up (Unit Stores)
Column No.	50	51	52	53	50a	53a
Formula	Ra-Wa / Ra	Ru-Wu / Ru	Ru-Ju / Ru	Ju-Wu / Ru	Ra-Wa / Wa	Ju-Wu / Wu
Symbol	Mta	Mtu	Mru	Mju	..	..
Commodity:	Per cent	Per cent	Per cent	Per cent	Per cent	Per cent
Northern potatoes	37	38	32	6	59	10
Southern potatoes	38[1]	39[1]	33[1]	6	62	13
California oranges	41	42	35	7	69	12
Peaches	45	45	36	9	80	17
Sweet potatoes	45	46	39	7	80	14
Cantaloupes	46	47	39	8	86	17
Boxed apples	46	47	36	11	87	22
Southern cabbage	48	48	37	11	91	20
Barreled apples	49	50	42	8	95	15
Eastern lettuce	51	52	39	13	105	26
Western lettuce	52	53	45	8	109	16
Yellow onions	53	53	46	7	111	16
Northern cabbage	58	58	49	9	139	23
White onions	63	64	52	12	167	..
Weighted mean	44.6	45.4	37.3	8.1[2]		

[1] Based on 12 months' data, 1923.

[2] Excluding white onions.

STORE TYPE COMPARISONS (GROCERY & FRUIT-VEGETABLE UNIT STORES)

	Number of Units Per Car	Price Per Unit					
		Mean Retail Price Per Unit (Grocery Stores)	Mean Retail Price Per Unit (Fruit-Vegetable Stores)	Mean Wholesale Price Per Unit (Grocery Stores)	Mean Wholesale Price Per Unit (Fruit-Vegetable Stores)	Mean Jobbers' Price Per Unit (Grocery Stores)	Mean Jobbers' Price Per Unit (Fruit-Vegetable Stores)
Column No.	54	55	56	57	58	59	60
Formula	..	..	..	..	..	..	..
Symbol	N	Rg	Rf	Wg	Wf	Jg	Jf
Commodity:	Units	Dollars	Dollars	Dollars	Dollars	Dollars	Dollars
Northern potatoes	400	4.11	3.97	2.44	2.49	2.74	2.73
Southern potatoes	330	9.31	8.85	5.96	5.95	7.59	6.72
California oranges	415	8.13	8.23	4.97	4.80	5.50	5.39
Peaches	500	4.18	3.91	2.24	2.15	2.63	2.53
Sweet potatoes	225	8.69	8.37	4.28	4.64	4.91	5.23
Cantaloupes	340	5.19	4.33	2.63	2.32	3.19	2.66
Boxed apples	750	4.64	4.43	2.42	2.35	2.90	2.87
Southern cabbage	210	8.68	8.61	4.34	4.59	5.54	5.39
Barreled apples	175	11.59	10.88	5.60	5.54	6.57	6.35
Eastern lettuce	400	4.84	4.44	2.30	2.17	2.93	2.72
Western lettuce	320	7.35	7.08	3.31	3.37	3.85	3.91
Yellow onions	250	7.23	6.64	3.31	3.12	3.82	3.61
Northern cabbage	300	4.94	4.81	2.02	2.01	2.54	2.46
White onions	250	9.60	8.62	3.40	3.17	4.45	4.22

STORE TYPE COMPARISONS (GROCERY & FRUIT-VEGETABLE UNIT STORES)

	Value Per Car					
	Mean Retail Value Per Car (Grocery Stores)	Mean Retail-Value Per Car (Fruit-Vegetable Stores)	Mean Wholesale Value Per Car (Grocery Stores)	Mean Wholesale Value Per Car (Fruit-Vegetable Stores)	Mean Jobbers' Value Per Car (Grocery Stores)	Mean Jobbers' Value Per Car (Fruit-Vegetable Stores)
Column No.	61	62	63	64	65	66
Formula	NRg	NRf	NWg	NWf	NJg	MJf
Symbol	Vrg	Vrf	Vwg	Vwf	Vjg	Vjf
Commodity:	Dollars	Dollars	Dollars	Dollars	Dollars	Dollars
Northern potatoes	1645	1590	975	995	1095	1090
Southern potatoes	3070	2920	1965	1965	2505	2220
California oranges	3625	3415	2065	1990	2280	2235
Peaches	2090	1955	1120	1075	1315	1265
Sweet potatoes	1955	1885	965	1045	1105	1175
Cantaloupes	1765	1470	895	790	1085	905
Boxed apples	3480	3325	1815	1765	2175	2155
Southern cabbage	1825	1810	910	965	1165	1130
Barreled apples	2030	1905	980	970	1150	1110
Eastern lettuce	1935	1775	920	870	1170	1090
Western lettuce	2350	2265	1060	1080	1230	1250
Yellow onions	1810	1660	830	780	955	905
Northern cabbage	1480	1445	605	605	760	740
White onions	2400	2155	850	795	1115	1055
Weighted mean	2275	2145	1220	1200	1445	1370

STORE TYPE COMPARISONS (GROCERY & FRUIT-VEGETABLE UNIT STORES)

	Spread Per Car					
	Total Spread (Grocery Stores)	Total Spread (Fruit-Vegetable Stores)	Retailer's Spread (Grocery Stores)	Retailer's Spread (Fruit-Vegetable Stores)	Jobber's Spread (Grocery Stores)	Jobber's Spread (Fruit-Vegetable Stores)
Column No.	67	68	69	70	71	72
Formula	Vrg-Vwg	Vrf-Vwf	Vrg-Vjg	Vrf-Vjf	Vjg-Vwg	Vjf-Vwf
Symbol	Ctg	Ctf	Crg	Crf	Cjg	Cjf
Commodity:	Dollars	Dollars	Dollars	Dollars	Dollars	Dollars
Northern potatoes	610	595	550	500	120	95
Southern potatoes	1105	955	565	700	540	255
California oranges	1560	1425	1340	1180	220	245
Peaches	970	880	775	690	195	190
Sweet potatoes	990	840	850	710	140	130
Cantaloupes	870	680	680	565	190	115
Boxed apples	1665	1560	1305	1170	360	390
Southern cabbage	915	845	660	680	255	165
Barreled apples	1050	935	880	795	170	140
Eastern lettuce	1015	905	765	685	250	220
Western lettuce	1290	1185	1120	1015	170	170
Yellow onions	980	880	855	755	125	125
Northern cabbage	875	840	720	705	155	135
White onions	1550	1360	1285	1100	265	260
Weighted mean	1055	945	830	775	225	170

STORE TYPE COMPARISONS (GROCERY & FRUIT-VEGETABLE STORES)

	Percentage Margin (Cents of Consumer's Dollar)					
	Total Margin (Grocery Stores)	Total Margin (Fruit and Vegetable Stores)	Retailer's Margin (Grocery Stores)	Retailer' Margin (Fruit and Vegetable Stores)	Jobber's Margin (Grocery Stores)	Jobber's Margin (Fruit and Vegetable Stores)
Column No.	73	74	75	76	77	78
Formula	$\frac{Rg-Wg}{Rg}$	$\frac{Rf-Wf}{Rf}$	$\frac{Rg-Jg}{Rg}$	$\frac{Rf-Jf}{Rf}$	$\frac{Jg-Wg}{Rg}$	$\frac{Jf-Wf}{Rf}$
Symbol	Mtg	Mtf	Mrg	Mrf	Mjg	Mjf
Commodity:	Per cent	Per cent	Per cent	Per cent	Per cent	Per cent
Northern potatoes	41	37	33	31	8	6
Southern potatoes	36	33	19	24	17	9
California oranges ...	43	42	37	35	6	7
Peaches	46	45	37	35	9	10
Sweet potatoes	51	45	44	38	7	7
Cantaloupes	49	46	39	39	10	7
Boxed apples	48	47	38	35	10	12
Southern cabbage	50	47	36	37	14	10
Barreled apples	52	49	43	42	9	7
Eastern lettuce	53	51	40	39	13	12
Western lettuce	55	53	48	45	7	8
Yellow onions	54	53	47	46	7	7
Northern cabbage	59	58	49	49	10	9
White onions	65	63	54	51	11	12
Weighted mean	46	44	36	36	10	8

STORE TYPE COMPARISONS (CHAIN STORES)

	Price Per Unit		Value Per Car		Spread Per Car	Percentage Margin
	Mean Retail Price Per Unit (Chain Stores)	Mean Wholesale Price Per Unit (Chain Stores)	Mean Retail Value Per Car (Chain Stores)	Mean Wholesale Value Per Car (Chain Stores)	Total Spread (Chain Stores)	Total Margin (Chain Stores) Cents of Consumer's Dollar
Column No.	79	80	81	82	83	84
Formula	..	..	NRc	NWc	Vrc-Vwc	$\frac{Rc-Wc}{Rc}$
Symbol	Rc	Wc	Vrc	VWc	Ctc	Mtc
Commodity:	Dollars	Dollars	Dollars	Dollars	Dollars	Per cent
Northern potatoes	2.89	2.36	1155	945	210	18
Southern potatoes [1]	..	(4.79)	(2150)	(1580)	(570)	(27)
California oranges	7.10	5.00	2945	2075	870	30
Peaches	3.84	2.37	1920	1185	735	38
Sweet potatoes	5.38	3.90	1210	880	330	28
Cantaloupes	4.80	2.97	1630	1010	620	38
Boxed apples	3.44	2.09	2580	1570	1010	39
Southern cabbage	6.94	3.69	1455	775	680	47
Barreled apples	8.58	5.38	1500	930	570	37
Eastern lettuce	3.56	1.82	1425	730	695	49
Western lettuce	6.19	3.50	1980	1120	860	44
Yellow onions	5.91	3.22	1480	805	675	46
Northern cabbage	3.56	1.63	1070	490	580	54
White onions	6.65	3.14	1660	785	875	53
Weighted mean	..	..	1735	1140	595	34

[1] Twelve months' prices.

ANALYSIS OF MANAGEMENT AND SERVICE POLICY (UNIT STORES AND CHAIN STORES)

	All Stores	Unit Stores	Credit-Delivery Unit Stores	Cash-Delivery Unit Stores	Cash-Carry Unit Stores	All Chain Stores	Cash-Delivery Chain Stores	Cash-Carry Chain Stores
Column No.	101	102	103	104	105	106	107	108
Formula	..	..	..	..	..	..	..	..
Symbol	Ara	Aru	Aru1	Aru2	Aru3	Arc	Arc2	Arc3
Commodity:	Number of Retail Price Quotations							
Northern potatoes	1650	1399	833	457	109	251	174	77
California oranges	2064	1843	1109	631	103	221	150	71
Sweet potatoes	1281	1148	698	387	63	133	86	47
Boxed apples	1453	1285	811	367	107	168	131	37
Barreled apples	1317	1184	706	389	89	133	88	45
Eastern lettuce	1331	1219	775	391	53	112	65	47
Yellow onions	1806	1524	903	515	106	282	184	98
Total	10902	9602	5835	3137	630	1300	878	422
14 commodity totals	14806	13115	7935	4339	841	1691	1105	586

ANALYSIS OF MANAGEMENT AND SERVICE POLICY (UNIT STORES AND CHAIN STORES)

	Mean Retail Price Per Unit							
	Basic Physical Unit	Unit Stores	Credit-Delivery Unit Stores	Cash-Delivery Unit Stores	Cash-Carry Unit Stores	All Chain Stores	Cash-Delivery Chain Stores	Cash-Carry Chain Stores
Column No.	109	110	111	112	113	114	115	116
Formula	..	..	..	..	..	..	..	..
Symbol	U	Ru	Ru1	Ru2	Ru3	Rc	Rc2	Rc3
Commodity:	Package	Dollars	Dollars	Dollars	Dollars	Dollars	Dollars	Dollars
Northern potatoes	cwt.	4.01	4.09	3.98	3.77	2.89	2.89	2.91
California oranges	box	8.37	8.87	7.83	7.23	7.10	7.09	7.11
Sweet potatoes	cwt.	8.44	9.03	7.77	5.96	5.38	5.75	4.70
Boxed apples	box	4.47	4.66	4.28	4.04	3.44	3.41	3.48
Barreled apples	bbl.	11.06	11.58	10.62	9.90	8.58	8.81	8.11
Eastern lettuce	3.dz. hpr.	4.55	4.78	4.29	4.43	3.56	3.46	3.70
Yellow onions	cwt.	6.80	7.07	6.77	6.16	5.91	5.76	6.22

ANALYSIS OF MANAGEMENT AND SERVICE POLICY (UNIT STORES AND CHAIN STORES)

	Mean Wholesale Price Per Unit						
	Unit Stores	Credit-Delivery Unit Stores	Cash-Delivery Unit Stores	Cash-Carry Unit Stores	All Chain Stores	Cash-Delivery Chain Stores	Cash-Carry Chain Stores
Column No.	117	118	119	120	121	122	123
Formula	..	..	..	..	..	..	..
Symbol	Wu	Wu1	Wu2	Wu3	Wc	Wc2	Wc3
Commodity:	Dollars	Dollars	Dollars	Dollars	Dollars	Dollars	Dollars
Northern potatoes	2.48	2.47	2.52	2.27	2.36	2.38	2.31
California oranges	4.84	4.93	4.79	4.86	5.00	5.02	4.96
Sweet potatoes	4.54	4.63	4.16	3.86	3.90	4.26	3.24
Boxed apples	2.37	2.41	2.35	2.25	2.09	2.09	2.11
Barreled apples	5.56	5.59	5.61	5.16	5.38	5.35	5.46
Eastern lettuce	2.20	2.30	2.18	2.21	1.82	1.83	1.81
Yellow onions	3.17	3.19	3.29	3.17	3.22	3.10	3.44

ANALYSIS OF MANAGEMENT AND SERVICE POLICY (UNIT STORES AND CHAIN STORES)

	Number of Units Per Car	Mean Retail Value Per Car						
		Unit Stores	Credit-Delivery Unit Stores	Cash-Delivery Unit Stores	Cash-Carry Unit Stores	All Chain Stores	Cash-Delivery Chain Stores	Cash-Carry Chain Stores
Column No.	124	125	126	127	128	129	130	131
Formula	..	NRu	NRu1	NRu2	NRu3	NRc	NRc2	NRc3
Symbol	N	Vru	Vru1	Vru2	Vru3	Vrc	Vrc2	Vru3
Commodity:	Number	Dollars	Dollars	Dollars	Dollars	Dollars	Dollars	Dollars
Northern potatoes	400	1605	1635	1590	1510	1155	1155	1165
California oranges ...	415	3475	2680	3250	3000	2945	2940	2950
Sweet potatoes	225	1900	2030	1750	1340	1210	1295	1060
Boxed apples	750	3355	3495	3210	3030	2580	2560	2610
Barreled apples	175	1935	2025	1860	1735	1500	1540	1420
Eastern lettuce	400	1820	1910	1715	1770	1425	1385	1480
Yellow onions	250	1700	1770	1695	1540	1480	1440	1555
Weighted means (7 commodities)	....	2180	2275	2095	1960	1700	1700	1700
Weighted means (14 commodities) ...	....	2105	....	....	....	1735	....	....

ANALYSIS OF MANAGEMENT AND SERVICE POLICY (UNIT STORES AND CHAIN STORES)

	Mean Wholesale Value Per Car						
	Unit Stores	Credit-Delivery Unit Stores	Cash-Delivery Unit Stores	Cash-Carry Unit Stores	All Chain Stores	Cash-Delivery Chain Stores	Cash-Carry Chain Stores
Column No.	132	133	134	135	136	137	138
Formula	NWu	NWu1	NWu2	NWu3	NWc	NWc2	NWc3
Symbol	Vwu	Vwu1	Vwu2	Vwu3	Vwc	Vwc2	Vwc3
Commodity:	Dollars	Dollars	Dollars	Dollars	Dollars	Dollars	Dollars
Northern potatoes	990	990	1010	910	945	950	925
California oranges	2010	2045	1990	2015	2075	2085	2060
Sweet potatoes	1020	1040	935	870	880	960	730
Boxed apples	1780	1810	1765	1690	1570	1570	1585
Barreled apples	975	980	980	905	930	935	955
Eastern lettuce	880	930	870	885	730	730	725
Yellow onions	795	800	825	795	805	775	860
Weighted means (7 commodities)	1185	1200	1190	1135	1130	1135	1125
Weighted means (14 commodities)	1150	....	....	....	1140	....	....

ANALYSIS OF MANAGEMENT AND SERVICE POLICY (UNIT STORES AND CHAIN STORES)

	Spread Per Car				
	All Unit Stores	Credit-Delivery Unit Stores	Cash-Delivery Unit Stores	Cash-Carry Unit Stores	All Chain Stores
Column No.	139	140	141	142	143
Formula	Vru-Vwu	Vru1-Vwu1	Vru2-Vwu2	Vru3-Vwu3	Vrc-Vwc
Symbol	Ctu	Ctu1	Ctu2	Ctu3	Ctc
Commodity:	Dollars	Dollars	Dollars	Dollars	Dollars
Northern potatoes	615	645	580	600	210
California oranges	1465	1635	1260	985	870
Sweet potatoes	880	990	815	470	330
Boxed apples	1575	1685	1445	1340	1010
Barreled apples	960	1045	880	830	570
Eastern lettuce	940	990	845	885	695
Yellow onions	905	970	870	745	675
Weighted means (7 commodities)	995	1070	905	825	570
Weighted means (14 commodities)	955	....	....	....	595

Analysis of Management and Service Policy (Unit Stores and Chain Stores)

	Total Percentage Margin							
	All Stores	All Unit Stores	Credit-Delivery Unit Stores	Cash-Delivery Unit Stores	Cash-Carry Unit Stores	All Chain Stores	Cash-Delivery Chain Stores	Cash-Carry Chain Stores
Column No.	144	145	146	147	148	149	150	151
Formula	(Ra-Wa)/Wa	Ctu/Vru	Ctu1/Vru1	Ctu2/Vru2	Ctu3/Vru3	Ctc/Vrc	Ctc2/Vrc2	Ctc3/Vrc3
Symbol	Mta	Mtu	Mtu1	Mtu2	Mtu3	Mtc	Mtc2	Mtc3
Commodity:	Per cent	Per cent	Per cent	Per cent	Per cent	Per cent	Per cent	Per cent
Northern potatoes	37	38	39	36	40	18	18	21
California oranges	41	42	44	39	33	30	29	30
Sweet potatoes	45	46	49	47	35	28	26	31
Boxed apples	46	47	48	45	44	39	39	39
Barreled apples	49	50	52	47	48	37	39	33
Eastern lettuce	51	52	52	49	50	49	47	51
Yellow onions	53	53	55	51	48	46	46	45
Weighted means (7 commodities)	44	45	47	43	42	33	33	33
Weighted means (14 commodities)	45	45	46	43	41	34	..	..

ANALYSIS OF MANAGEMENT AND SERVICE POLICY (UNIT STORES AND CHAIN STORES)

	Mean Number of Retail Sales Per Car	Mean Retail Value Per Standard Retail Sale				
		All Unit Stores	Credit-Delivery Unit Stores	Cash-Delivery Unit Stores	Cash-Carry Unit Stores	All Chain Stores
Column No.	152	153	154	155	156	157
Formula	..	$\frac{Vru}{Sr}$	$\frac{Vru1}{Sr}$	$\frac{Vru2}{Sr}$	$\frac{Vru3}{Sr}$	$\frac{Vrc}{Sr}$
Symbol	Sr	Zru	Zru1	Zru2	Zru3	Zrc
Commodity:	Sales	Cents	Cents	Cents	Cents	Cents
Northern potatoes	5805	27.7	28.2	27.4	26.0	19.9
California oranges	12380	28.1	29.7	26.3	24.2	23.8
Sweet potatoes	7345	25.9	27.6	23.8	18.2	16.5
Boxed apples	13220	25.4	26.4	24.3	22.9	19.5
Barreled apples	7855	24.6	25.8	23.7	22.1	19.1
Eastern lettuce	7765	23.4	24.6	22.1	22.8	18.4
Yellow onions	7250	23.5	24.4	23.4	21.2	20.4
Weighted means (7 commodities)	8405	25.9	27.0	24.9	23.3	20.2
Weighted means (14 commodities)	....	25.9	..	..	..	..

ANALYSIS OF MANAGEMENT AND SERVICE POLICY (UNIT STORES AND CHAIN STORES)

	Spread Per Standard Retail Sale				
	All Unit Stores	Credit-Delivery Unit Stores	Cash-Delivery Unit Stores	Cash-Carry Unit Stores	All Chain Stores
Column No.	158	159	160	161	162
Formula	$\frac{Ctu}{Sr}$	$\frac{Ctu1}{Sr}$	$\frac{Ctu2}{Sr}$	$\frac{Ctu3}{Sr}$	$\frac{Ctc}{Sr}$
Symbol	Dtu	Dtu1	Dtu2	Dtu3	Dtc
Commodity:	Cents	Cents	Cents	Cents	Cents
Northern potatoes	10.6	11.1	10.0	10.3	3.6
California oranges	11.8	13.2	10.2	8.0	7.0
Sweet potatoes	12.0	13.5	11.1	6.4	4.4
Boxed apples	11.9	12.7	10.9	10.1	7.6
Barreled apples	12.2	13.3	11.2	10.6	7.3
Eastern lettuce	12.1	12.7	10.9	11.4	9.0
Yellow onions	12.5	13.4	12.0	10.3	9.3
Weighted mean [1]	(11.8)	(12.8)	(10.8)	(9.8)	(6.8)

[1] The parentheses on pp. 161 and 163 indicate that the weighted figures were derived by dividing the respective mean spreads per car and differentials per car by the weighted mean number of retail sales per car—8405:

ANALYSIS OF MANAGEMENT AND SERVICE POLICY (UNIT STORES AND CHAIN STORES)

	Differential in Spread Per Car				
	Chain Store Gross	Chain Store Net	"Cash-carry"	"Cash"	"Carry"
Column No.	163	164	165	166	167
Formula	Ctu-Ctc	Ctu3-Ctc	Ctu1-Ctu3	Ctu1-Ctu2	Ctu2-Ctu3
Symbol	Huc	Hu3c	Hu1u3	Hu1u2	Hu2u3
Commodity:	Dollars	Dollars	Dollars	Dollars	Dollars
Northern potatoes	405	390	45	65	—20
California oranges	595	115	650	375	275
Sweet potatoes	550	140	520	175	345
Boxed apples	565	330	345	240	105
Barreled apples	390	260	215	165	50
Eastern lettuce	245	190	105	145	—40
Yellow onions	230	70	225	100	125
Weighted mean	425	255	250	170	80
Weighted average deviation	100	100	160	80	95
Weighted average deviation as percentage of weighted mean	(24%)	(39%)	(64%)	(47%)	(119%)

ANALYSIS OF MANAGEMENT AND SERVICE POLICY (UNIT STORES AND CHAIN STORES)

	Differential in Value of Standard Retail Sale (Adjusted)				
	Chain Store Gross	Chain Store Net	"Cash-Carry"	"Cash"	"Carry"
Column No.	168	169	170	171	172
Formula	Huc / Sr	Hu3c / Sr	Hu1u3 / Sr	Hu1u2 / Sr	Hu2u3 / Sr
Symbol	Kuc	Ku3c	Ku1u3	Ku1u2	Ku2u3
Commodity:	Cents	Cents	Cents	Cents	Cents
Northern potatoes	7.0	6.7	.8	1.1	—.3
California oranges ...	4.8	.9	5.2	3.0	2.2
Sweet potatoes	7.5	1.9	7.1	2.4	4.7
Boxed apples	4.3	2.5	2.6	1.8	.8
Barreled apples	5.0	3.3	2.7	2.1	.6
Eastern lettuce	3.2	2.4	1.4	1.9	—.5
Yellow onions	3.2	1.0	3.1	1.4	1.7
Weighted mean [1]	(5.0)	(3.0)	(3.0)	(2.0)	(1.0)

[1] See footnote, page 161.

Tests of Validity of Jobbers' and Wholesalers' Quotations as Representative of Actual Sales

(1) A check of the validity of dealers' quotations as representative of actual sales was afforded by comparing sales records of individual jobbers in two markets on a given date with their price quotations, for four seasonal commodities. The differences between quotations and sales figures, and the variance as a percentage of the latter, were as follows:

NEWARK JOBBER—MAY 18, 1923

	New Potatoes (bbl.)	Onions (cwt.)	Lettuce (hamper)	Apples (bbl.)
Quotation	$8.50	$2.88	$5.25	$8.50
Typical Sale Price	9.00	3.00	4.50	9.00
Difference	—.50	—.12	+.75	—.50
Percentage Variance	—5.6%	—4.%	+16.7%	—5.6%

WALLABOUT JOBBER—JUNE 15, 1923

	New Potatoes (bbl.)	Onions (cwt.)	Lettuce (hamper)	Apples (bbl.)
Quotation	$6.50	$3.25	$2.00	$12.50
Typical Sale Price	6.50	3.25	1.88	12.75
Difference	0	0	+.12	—.25
Percentage Variance	0	0	+6%	—2%

(2) A test of the validity of figures used in the study to represent quotations from individual jobbers in Gansevoort, Harlem, Wallabout and Newark Markets on a typical market day, for each of four commodities, showed an average deviation of quotations around the figure used ranging from 27 cents a hundredweight for onions to 46 cents a hamper for lettuce. As percentages of the typical figure, the average deviations around it were: potatoes 3.3%, apples 6.7%, onions 8.3%, lettuce 13.1%. Following are the data:

	New Potatoes	Yellow Onions	Florida Lettuce	Baldwin Apples
Date	Apr. 27, 1923	Mar. 2, 1923	Mar. 2, 1923	Mar. 2, 1923
Number of Qnotations	8	16	13	13
Price Range	\$9.50 to \$11 per bbl	\$2.50 to \$3.75 per cwt.	\$2.00 to \$4.50 per hamper	\$4.00 to \$7.00 per bbl.
Mean Price	10.22	3.15	3.38	5.97
Modal Price	10.00	..	..	6.00
Figure Used	10.00	3.25	3.50	6.00
Average Deviation. Around Figure Used	.34 (3.3%)	.27 (8.3%)	.46 (13.1%)	.40 (6.7%)

(3) To illustrate the accuracy of the official figures of the U. S. Department of Agriculture as representative of transactions in the wholesale market, data of purchases by a Newark jobber in the New York wholesale market on four Fridays in May, 1923, were checked against the official figures for the same dates. The differences found between the jobber's typical purchase price and the official quotation on each date were:

	New Potatoes	Onions	Lettuce	Baldwin Apples
	(bbl.)	(cwt.)	(hamper)	(bbl.)
May 4	..	..	.25	0
May 11	.05	.08	..	..
May 18	.70	..	.13	..
May 25	.42	..	..	..
Average Percentage difference	4-5%	3%	5%	..

INDEX

www.ingramcontent.com/pod-product-compliance
Lightning Source LLC
LaVergne TN
LVHW021357110826
845150LV00007B/1692

* 9 7 8 1 4 2 5 5 1 4 4 5 7 *